The Yellow Ruff
&
THE SCARLET LETTER

Alfred S. Reid, a native of Florida, was
educated at the University of Miami (A.B.,
1948) and the University of Florida (M.A.,
1950; Ph.D., 1952). Formerly an instructor
in English at Trinity College, Connecticut,
Dr. Reid has recently been appointed to the
faculty of Furman University.

The Yellow Ruff

&

THE SCARLET LETTER

A
Source
of
Hawthorne's Novel

by

ALFRED S. REID

UNIVERSITY OF FLORIDA PRESS
GAINESVILLE ~ 1955

To

Professor Harry R. Warfel

A UNIVERSITY OF FLORIDA PRESS BOOK

COPYRIGHT, 1955, BY THE UNIVERSITY OF FLORIDA

Library of Congress Catalogue Card No. 55-9943

10-27-55

MANUFACTURED BY THE RECORD PRESS, INCORPORATED
ST. AUGUSTINE, FLORIDA

PREFACE

THE THEORY set forth in this book—that Hawthorne's *The Scarlet Letter* grew from the fertilization of a story-germ by an actual case of adultery, revenge, murder, and concealed sin—originated in a passing curiosity about the name of the minister. The surnames of two major characters in the novel coincide with the names of prominent figures in seventeenth-century history. Was there also a historical Dimmesdale? The results of that inquiry now comprise parts of Chapters X and XII of this study. Meanwhile, the names of bona fide historical persons cited in the novel having drawn my attention, I pursued them through the books that Hawthorne read during the summer and autumn of 1849. One cluster of names led to literature reporting a sordid criminal case, which struck me as bearing a crude but fascinating likeness to Hawthorne's story; and after a closer examination of this literature I concluded that I had unearthed the body of facts which were not merely alluded to by Hawthorne but which possibly sprang into his mental structure and thence into the novel during the formative stages of that work.

This book explores the possibilities of this theory. Two factors ultimately determined the organization of material. One was the hope of keeping the novel as inviolate during its analysis as is possible in a source study. The other was the desire of grouping the evidence in such a way as to stimulate interpretation. The organizing principle, therefore, is the showing of minute parallels between elements in the novel and the case, first as to story, then characters, setting, and style. An introductory chapter sketches the outline of the case, describes the works that report it, and presents preliminary evidence that validates these works as pos-

v

Preface

sible sources of the novel. A concluding chapter summarizes the principal arguments and discusses the implications that arise about Hawthorne's creative process, about the genesis and evolution of the novel, and about the meaning of the novel in relation to Hawthorne's art. By viewing the independent sources that narrate the crime as a single reservoir of information, this method of organization destroys the unity of the several suggested sources, to which the reader must go to get the full flavor of their antiquarian and moral nature. But I believe that this approach, in accord with new critical canons, keeps the emphasis on the novel rather than on the sources, lays foundations for future studies of these traditional critical divisions of the novel, and offers insights into Hawthorne's mental processes.

I wish to acknowledge the assistance given me by Mrs. Willie Kate Bloomfield of the University of Florida Library and that by Professors Denver E. Baughan, J. E. Congleton, Ants Oras, Delton L. Scudder, and Harry R. Warfel of the University of Florida faculty. I am especially grateful to Professor Warfel for his teaching that inspired this research and for his critical judgment and patient encouragement that stimulated its completion; and I am deeply indebted to my wife Nathalie for her assistance in many ways.

ALFRED S. REID

Trinity College
Hartford, Connecticut
September, 1954

vi

CONTENTS

c~~~~ 1 ~~~~

TWO SUGGESTIVE ALLUSIONS

I~N~ "The Custom House," in a
passage which no one takes seriously, Hawthorne ascribes the basic
outline of *The Scarlet Letter* to a manuscript narration of Puritan
New England penned by Jonathan Pue (p. 51).* More important,
however, are two allusions in the novel wherein he unobtrusively
compares characters of his creation to persons who were central
actors in a court intrigue during the reign of King James the First
of England. This episode was the murder of Sir Thomas Overbury
in the Tower of London in 1613. Hawthorne cites the names of
Overbury, Doctor Simon Forman, and Mistress Anne Turner, and
he mentions another person in the case without calling his name.
In one of these allusions the novelist thus identifies Roger Chillingworth: "There was an aged handicraftsman, it is true, who had
been a citizen of London at the period of Sir Thomas Overbury's
murder, now some thirty years agone; he testified to having seen
the physician, under some other name, which the narrator of the
story had now forgotten, in company with Doctor Forman, the
famous old conjuror, who was implicated in the affair of Overbury" (pp. 155-156). The second allusion occurs in a description
of Mistress Hibbins' dress: "She made a very grand appearance;
having on a high headdress, a rich gown of velvet, and a ruff done
up with the famous yellow starch, of which Ann Turner, her

---

*Parenthetical page references to *The Scarlet Letter* are to Volume V of the
Riverside Edition (1890) of Hawthorne's works.

especial friend, had taught her the secret, before this last good lady had been hanged for Sir Thomas Overbury's murder" (p. 264).

A close study of several documents relating to the Overbury affair, as Hawthorne called it, reveals many striking parallels between the facts of that case and the novel. Could there be any connection between this murder and the story of *The Scarlet Letter?* To indicate how this question might be answered, it will be necessary first to outline the incidents in the Overbury murder, to describe several works relating to it, to present evidence validating Hawthorne's knowledge of these works, and to make a detailed comparison between the novel and these accounts of the case.

The Scarlet Letter need not be retold here, but the sequence of events in the Overbury murder is less widely known and far more complicated. The affair was set in motion in 1606 by a forced marriage of convenience between the children of influential courtly families, Frances Howard, aged 13, and Robert Devereux, Earl of Essex, aged 14. Deemed too young to live with his still more youthful wife, Robert was sent on a grand tour of the continent, and in his absence, Lady Frances fell in love with Robert Carr, Viscount of Rochester and King James's rising favorite. Carr, who had early in his career cultivated the friendship of Sir Thomas Overbury, an aspiring courtier, had gained royal favor largely because of Overbury's prudent counsel. At first, Overbury had countenanced and even encouraged his friend's adulterous liaison with the child bride of Essex, but on learning that Carr and Lady Frances were planning to marry, Overbury protested vigorously his friend's marriage to an unfaithful woman on the ground that she might in turn be unfaithful to her new husband. This intervention incurred the hatred of both Lady Frances and Carr, whose influential position enabled him to persuade King James to appoint Overbury to a foreign diplomatic assignment, a post he Janus-like advised Overbury to decline. When Overbury refused to accept the appointment, as Carr had hoped, the young knight was promptly committed to the Tower—this was in April, 1613—thus opening the way for the lovers to proceed with plans to obtain Lady Frances' divorce from Lord Essex. While a commission was deciding her suit for divorce, she meanwhile was seeking a dastardly revenge on Overbury, whose knowledge of her conduct seemed to her the only obstacle to success and happiness. To further her ends, she solicited the aid of Mrs. Anne Turner, an unprincipled friend, who procured from a quack doctor, Simon Forman, and from other pretenders to occult arts, the formulae for poisonous compounds. For five months these agents of Lady Frances administered lethal concoctions to Overbury, in his food, in his medicine, and in choice tarts and jellies supposedly sent to him by Lady Frances herself. The smuggling of these poisons in to the prisoner had been made possible by an earlier act which placed Overbury under the strict surveillance of a specially appointed Lieutenant of the Tower, Jervase Helwyse, and by assigning an old servant in Mrs. Turner's home, Richard Weston, to be Overbury's personal attendant. Slowly these poisons began to take effect, and on September 15, 1613, a poisoned clyster finally brought about his death. A week later, Lady Frances was granted a divorce on the false charge of her husband's sexual impotence; and only three months afterwards, December 26, 1613, she and Carr, who now was the Earl of Somerset, were able to consummate their lust legally in marriage.

This plot of adultery, malice, and murder remained a secret for nearly two years. Accounts of how it was brought to light vary. One report says that James Franklin, one of the poisoners, exposed the plot during an illness in Holland. Another states that an apothecary's boy, who it seems had been bribed to administer the fatal clyster, revealed the strategem. Some persons suspected that the King himself had a share in the murder and instigated prosecution to rid himself of Carr for a new favorite, George Villiers. Another account gives credit to Jervase Helwyse for confessing the plot to Sir Ralph Winwood, the King's Secretary, because the jailer's connivance weighed heavily on his conscience. Despite this aura of mystery which enshrouds the whole affair, the actors in the tragedy were finally taken in custody, and the accomplices were brought to trial in October and November, 1615, were convicted, and were hanged. While awaiting trial in prison, Lady Frances gave birth to a baby girl, Anne Carr, and soon afterward, in May, 1616, Carr and his Countess were tried and were sentenced to death. Although later their punishments were lessened, and they were released from prison in January, 1622, they were still confined to certain designated houses until complete pardon was granted them just before King James's death in 1624.[1]

The outline of events in the Overbury affair presents, at first glance, several striking parallels with the novel. Each possesses salient features of adultery, deceitful revenge on a trusting friend, slow death, troubled conscience, prison birth of a baby girl, and banishment from society. In later chapters these parallels will be treated in full.

Hawthorne's allusions to Overbury and to several obscure persons involved in the murder, Anne Turner and Dr. Forman in particular, obviously show that Hawthorne was acquainted with the case. Three accounts of the crime, as later evidence will seek to demonstrate in detail, seem to have been the sources of most of Hawthorne's knowledge about it. These three accounts are an anonymous prose narration, "The Five Years of King James" (1643); a poem, entitled "Sir Thomas Overbury's Vision" (1616), by an obscure London poet named Richard Niccols (1584-1616) on the trials of the accomplices; and the criminal proceedings in the *State Trials*. The tract and the poem are included among the antiquarian contents of *The Harleian Miscellany*, a work which Hawthorne used in 1828 and again in November and December, 1849, about the time he was writing the novel.[2] *The Miscellany* is a "Collection of Scarce, Curious, and Entertaining Pamphlets and Tracts," compiled from the library of Robert Harley, the second Earl of Oxford, after his death in 1724.

Turn for a moment to these three versions of the case. The prose pamphlet, "The Five Years of King James, or, The Condition of the State of England, and the Relation It Had to Other Provinces," is of unknown authorship. The narrator, possibly a Puritan, characterizes the state of England during the early years of King James's reign. He fears that licentiousness and prodigality threaten to undermine the Commonwealth. To illustrate this widespread corruption of morals, he relates in vivid detail the Overbury scandal. He begins with King James's first recognition of Robert Carr, when at a court tilting match the youth fell from a horse, broke his leg, and grew thereafter into favor. He narrates the liaison between Carr and Lady Frances, Countess of Essex. He explains how the Countess, Mrs. Turner, and Dr. Forman used love powders to inflame Carr towards the Countess; while with other philters and waxen images they tried to debilitate Essex and bring about frigidity in him. He tells of the friendship between Carr and Overbury and how it turned to hatred. He describes the murderous plot on Overbury's life. He gives an account of Lady Frances' divorce suit, a summary of the trials of the murderers, their punishments, and the pardons of Carr and Lady Frances.

Frequently the author refers to other matters of state. He describes the tensions between the English and the Hollanders, the Scots, and the Irish. He mentions the marriage of Princess Elizabeth and the death of Prince Henry; he refers to the Gunpowder Plot and the Catholic danger; he tells of the imprisonment and death of Lady Arabella, King James's cousin, and of the execution of Sir Walter Raleigh. But the engrossing subject upon this larger canvas is the Overbury incident, which he paints in a quaint, gossipy style, far from the Attic ideal, repetitiously compounded of the rumors and opinions of the people on the scene.

A second important source of Hawthorne's knowledge of the Overbury affair may have been Richard Niccols' "Sir Thomas Overbury's Vision: with the Ghosts of Weston, Mistress Turner, the late Lieutenant of the Tower, and Franklin," an imaginative summation in verse of the thoughts of the accomplices who were executed for the murder of Overbury. Incorrectly called "Overbury's Vision," the poem is actually the dream vision of the author. Deeply moved by the trials, Niccols wrote the poem to vindicate the attacks on Overbury's character. The opening lines state that poison and foul wrong are the themes. Niccols describes the public forum where he has been among the thick of the throng witnessing the trials at Guildhall. He returns home and, in his sleep, dreams that the ghost of the poisoned knight enters his chamber and beckons him to follow. The ghost conducts him to Tower Hill and explains how he has been maliciously betrayed, imprisoned, and poisoned. Because of posthumous slanders on his character, he has left the grave to beg the poet's assistance in clearing his reputation. Niccols describes Traitor's Gate near where they stand. As the ghost and poet observe the gate, out of the prisoner's dock rises the ghost of Weston, who admits his guilt in Overbury's murder. Anne Turner's ghost follows, repents of her crime, points out the steps leading to her disgrace, and warns other women from following them. The ghost of Jervase Helwyse next appears, begging forgiveness and cautioning officials against temptations of bribery. Finally, Franklin's ghost rises and tells how greed and atheism led to his downfall. When the specters have returned to their graves, Overbury's ghost praises King James for his just punishment of the murderers. The dream ends, and, as Overbury had urged, Niccols awakes to write this vision.

The poet obviously attempts to vindicate the life of Sir Thomas Overbury and to curry King James's favor. His didactic aims are equally apparent. He warns his readers against the evils of court life: pride, vanity, overzealous ambition, obsequiousness, social climbing, atheism, and greedy acceptance of bribes. Niccols' plan is well conceived but awkwardly executed. A historical digression on crimes in the Tower mars its unity, and the heroic verse is at times little better than doggerel. Yet the poem is a contemporaneous reaction to the trials by an eyewitness. For its unique interpretations of the characters that it portrays, the "Vision" becomes an important document in the succeeding exposition of Hawthorne's imaginative assimilation of the Overbury materials.

Another important source of Hawthorne's information about the Overbury case may have been the criminal proceedings in the Star Chamber as collected in the *State Trials*. To be found here are the arraignments by the prosecution and the pleadings of the defendants; their sentences, their confessions, and their dying speeches at their executions; the divorce proceedings of Lady Frances; the royal pardons of Somerset and his Countess; Somerset's petitions for renewed favor; and the provisions of their final release from the Tower.

Two Suggestive Allusions

With the *State Trials*, as with *The Harleian Miscellany*, Hawthorne was on intimate terms that date back at least as far as 1832. He found the reading of its pages enchanting, as he told his friend, James T. Fields, the publisher of *The Scarlet Letter*, who relates:

Hearing him [Hawthorne] say once that the old English State Trials were enchanting reading, and knowing that he did not possess a copy of those heavy folios, I picked up a set one day in a book-shop and sent them to him. He often told me that he spent more hours over them and got more delectation out of them than tongue could tell, and he said, if five lives were vouchsafed to him, he could employ them all in writing stories out of those books. He had sketched, in his mind, several romances founded on the remarkable trials reported in the ancient volumes; and one day, I remember, he made my blood tingle by relating some of the situations he intended, if his life was spared, to weave into future romances.[3]

Elizabeth Hawthorne corroborates the evidence of Hawthorne's fondness for reading these reports of trials. In a letter to Fields in 1870 she wrote that of the works that her brother read during the "solitary years," 1825-1837, *The Gentleman's Magazine* and "6 vols. folio, of Howell's State Trials, he preferred to any others."[4]

Besides these works, Hawthorne knew additional books relating to the case or containing summaries of it. Michael Sparke's *The Narrative History of King James, for the First Fourteen Years* (1651) incorporates, as Part One, the whole of "The Five Years of King James." Much of the material on the case in the *State Trials* is duplicated in Part Two, titled "Truth Brought to Light by Time." Hawthorne borrowed this history from the Salem Athenaeum in 1827. Alfred John Kempe's *The Loseley Manuscripts* (1836) contains a historical sketch of the murder, some letters by the King's council regarding the prisoners Carr and Lady Frances, and an inventory of some personal effects of Carr and Mrs. Turner. Kempe collected these papers, belonging to James More Molyneux, from the muniment room at Loseley Hall in Surrey, England. The documents in the miscellany relate to history and biography, court entertainments, political missions, and particulars of domestic life. Kempe's purpose is to give a "very correct idea of the state of society and political government in the 16th and early part of the 17th centuries." Hawthorne borrowed this work from the Salem Athenaeum about the time he was working on the novel, October 9, 1849. A month later, November 6, 1849, he borrowed *The Harleian Miscellany*. He returned them on December 21, 1849, and a little more than a month later, February 3, 1850, he reported that he had finished the novel.[5]

Hawthorne could have known the Overbury affair from still other sources. He was acquainted with Sir Francis Bacon's works, which contain papers that relate to the case. Bacon, then Attorney General, participated in the trials of Carr and Lady Frances. Hawthorne cites Bacon in the novel, along with three other legal figures mentioned in the *State Trials*, Chief Justice Coke, who presided at the trials of the accomplices, and Finch and Noye (p. 131). Many histories of the Jacobean period appear on the list of Hawthorne's reading. In every one of them that has been available for this study, the Overbury murder, one of the great scandals of its day, is retold. The romancer knew those by Baker, Oldmixon, and Rapin-Thoyras; he had access in the Salem Athenaeum to others. He also knew John Britton's and E. W. Braley's *Memoirs of the Tower* (1830). He was acquainted with *Biographia Britannica; or, the Lives of . . . Eminent Persons . . . in Great Britain . . .* (1747-1766). Still other works on the Overbury affair, whose pages he may have turned, were in circulation before 1849. Thomas Birch's *The Court and Times of James the First* (1849) unfolds through the letters of John Chamberlain and other persons the social history of the age, and frequently the Overbury affair is mentioned. Andrew Amos' *The Great Oyer of Poisoning* (1846) is a massive historical and legal study of the case. Sir Walter Scott's *Secret History of the Court of James the First* (1811) includes a group of books on the age; one, Sir Anthony Weldon's *The Court and Character of King James* (1651), discusses the affair of Overbury in colorful fashion. Weldon's account is also carried in the footnotes of the *State Trials*. Arthur Wilson's *The History of Great Britain . . . Life and Reign of King James the*

8

First (1653) is the source of many details on the case mentioned by Kempe and other later narrators. Besides being versified by Niccols in 1616, the Overbury affair was dramatized twice in the eighteenth century, by Richard Savage and William Woodfall.[6]

There seems to be little doubt that Hawthorne was widely read in the histories and miscellaneous collections of the age of Elizabeth and James I. He was steeped in the *causes célèbres* that attracted the attention of the historians. One may find many allusions scattered throughout his tales to famous personages and events of the time. Lady Arabella Stuart, for instance, is mentioned in "Main Street" (1849), and "The Antique Ring" (1843) is based on the beheading at Queen Elizabeth's command of Lord Essex, the father of the Lord Essex involved in the Overbury scandal. Hawthorne gave the name *Jervase Helwyse*—the name of one of the actors in the Overbury tragedy—to a pale-faced secretary in "Lady Eleanor's Mantle." This coincidence would suggest that he adapted details from the Overbury affair as early as 1838; George P. Lathrop, however, cites a "Gervice Helwisse" in the Hawthorne family tree, and Hawthorne devotes a paragraph in his English journals to a discussion of this relative, "Gervase Elwes,"[7] so that this early use of the name may have been prompted by either circumstance, more likely by the latter. Nevertheless, the existence in Hawthorne's genealogical records of a man with a name identical to one in the Overbury case may very likely have attracted his attention more keenly to the Overbury affair.

The evidence suggests at this point a conclusion that the references to the Overbury affair arose not from a passing acquaintance with this crime, which Bacon called, for its sensational repercussions, second only to the Gunpowder Plot,[8] but that Hawthorne knew thoroughly the main facts of that affair and was deeply impressed, and possibly influenced, by the case. It may be stated further as a working hypothesis that the details of the Overbury murder were the most important pliable materials which crowded into Hawthorne's imagination as it wrought into a novel of adultery, revenge, and conscience a static image of a woman wearing a scarlet letter.

9

Part One — Introduction

This idea for a tale about a guilty wearer of the letter A was suggested to Hawthorne's mind by a statute in Massachusetts colonial history. In 1704, the General Court of Massachusetts Bay passed a law providing that adulterers, "both Man and Woman," were not only to be placed on the gallows for an hour and to be scourged, but ever afterwards they were "to wear a Capital A of two inches long, of a contrary colour to the cloathes, sewed on their upper Garments, on the Back or Arm, in open view."[9] Hawthorne first used this suggestion in 1837 in "Endicott and the Red Cross." Standing with the other guilty ones being punished on the day that the red cross was removed from the ensign "was likewise a young woman, with no mean share of beauty, whose doom it was to wear the letter A on the breast of her gown. . . . Sporting with her infamy, the lost and desperate creature had embroidered the fatal token in scarlet cloth, with golden thread and the nicest art of needlework."[10] Seven years later a note in his journal proposed the building of an entire tale on "the life of a woman, who, by the old colony law, was condemned always to wear the letter A, sewed on her garment, in token of her having committed adultery."[11]

From this simple, static image that is known to have been the original inspiration for *The Scarlet Letter*, Hawthorne evolved a novel as complex as life and as dynamic as drama. That he could set this image into motion is certainly a mystery. Professor John Livingston Lowes has described the mysterious process by which Coleridge's imagination imposed on chaotic materials the order that is "The Rime of the Ancient Mariner" and "Kubla Khan."[12] A corresponding process, one may assume, took place in Hawthorne's imagination in the creation of *The Scarlet Letter*. All his reading, his experience, his thought surely entered into its composition, because the imaginaton, as Professor Lowes clearly demonstrated, cannot operate on a void. Somewhere there exist other materials than the Massachusetts law that must have supplied Hawthorne's imagination with the details to energize this symbol. The novelist's two allusions to Overbury's murder certify that he knew about this crime. At first glance, broad similarities between the case and the novel appear. Discussions of the case recurred frequently enough in his reading to have given him a thorough grounding in all its sordid details of adultery and vengeful murder. He was reading works that narrated the case at the time he wrote the novel. In the ensuing chapters, parallels of plot, characters, setting, and style between the novel and the literature of the Overbury murder will be pointed out. When this evidence has been presented, there should emerge more clearly an answer to the question proposed: Could materials from the Overbury affair have surged into Hawthorne's creative imagination to become shaped into *The Scarlet Letter?* Notice, first, parallels of plot.

 ~~~ 2 ~~~

ADULTERY & OSTRACISM

T HE SCARLET LETTER is the story of a disgraced young woman named Hester Prynne. The wife of an elderly physician, she is doomed for life to wear on her garment a scarlet letter as punishment for adultery. She is virtually ostracized from society by this symbol of guilt, but she repents her crime against Puritan society and against God's law and performs a lengthy penance. Her partner-in-crime, however, the Reverend Arthur Dimmesdale, keeps his sin a secret and slowly succumbs to the tortures of his conscience as well as to a mysterious revenge inflicted upon him by a malicious doctor of physic, Roger Chillingworth, who, unknown to the minister, is the betrayed husband.

The plot of the novel orginates in Hester Prynne's adultery with the Reverend Arthur Dimmesdale during her husband's absence. This sin, though it precedes the story told by Hawthorne, provides the initial situation from which arises the action of the novel. Two adulterous relationships appear in the narratives of the Overbury crime. The more prominent one is a triangle involving Lady Frances, the adulteress; Lord Essex, the husband; and Robert Carr, the fornicator. Frances Howard and Robert Devereux, young teen-agers who were married in 1606, were immediately separated. While Essex was traveling outside the country, Lady Frances noticed the accumulating honors of King James's rising favorite, Robert Carr. Unhappy in her marital union with Essex, she was "fired with a lustfull desire" toward Carr, with whom she held frequent rendezvous at secret places previously arranged.[1] She and Carr were assisted in their adulterous meetings by her great-uncle, the Earl of Northampton, and by her widowed sexual adviser, Anne Turner. The doors of both these panderers' homes stood open for the eager lovers. They met "in Mris. Turners house once between the houres of eleven and twelve, and at Hammersmith, and at divers times elsewhere."[2] This unlawful love led eventually to Lady Frances' divorce from Lord Essex and to marriage between her and Carr. No children, however, seem to have been born to the adulteress until after this latter marriage, although "it was vulgarly reported that shee had had a child in my Lords absence."[3]

The second adulterous liaison is one involving Anne Turner. This physician's widow was simultaneously engaged in an affair with one of the Prince's household, Arthur Manwaring, Clerk of the Pipe, and by him, it was related, "she had 3 children."[4] Seeking by force of magic to gain him for her husband, she solicited the conjuror Forman to help both her and Lady Frances in their passionate desires.

Both of these amours will need to be kept in mind by the reader during the following discussion, for, says the narrator, Lady Frances and Anne Turner were "neer of the . . . [same] disposition and temperature."[5] The fact that there are two adulteresses in the case and that Lady Frances had two husbands, though at different times in her life, will make still more confusing the discussion of parallels. It will be necessary for the sake of clarity to keep the several sets of relationships distinct, yet, at the same time, to allow them to amalgamate, as would have happened in an artist's imagination.

Hawthorne begins the action of the romance with the penalty that is being inflicted upon Hester by the Puritan tribunal. A throng of people are assembled in groups, first at the prison door and then in the market-place, to witness her shame. In one of these groups, a stern-featured matron exclaims: "What think ye, gossips? If the hussy stood up for judgment before us five, that are now here in a knot together, would she come off with

such a sentence as the worshipful magistrates have awarded?"
(P. 71.) As "self-constituted judges," remarks Hawthorne, they
pass judgment upon the malefactress. Only a young wife, holding
a child by the hand, and a man in the crowd express merciful
thoughts (p. 72). These dramatic details have striking parallels
in the introductory verses of Richard Niccols' "Sir Thomas Overbury's Vision," descriptive of a trial day at Guildhall:

> *Then did th' inconstant vulgar day by day,*
> *Like feathers in the wind, blown every way,*
> *Frequent the Forum; where, in thickest throng,*
> *I one amongst the rest did pass along*
> *To hear the judgment of the wise, and know*
> *That late black deed, the cause of mickle woe:*
> *But, from the reach of voice too far compell'd,*
> *That beast of many heads I there beheld,*
> *And did observe how every common drudge*
> *Assum'd the person of an aweful judge:*
>
> . . . .
>
> *Here four or five, that with the vulgar sort*
> *Will not impart their matters of import,*
> *Withdraw and whisper. . . .*
>
> . . . .
>
> *Here some excuse that which was most amiss;*
> *Others do there accuse, where no crime is,*
> *Accusing that which they excus'd anon,*
> *Inconstant people, never constant known.*[6]

Where Niccols stresses the fickleness of the people, Hawthorne
concentrates on a mood of severity. But in both descriptions the
situation is a legal proceeding. The market-place in the novel
agrees with the forum in the poem, and the knot of five parallels
the groups of four or five. In both scenes the people assume the
authority of judges, and in both there is a diversity of opinion.
The prison door opens and a beadle leads Hester forth to the
place of judgment in the market-place. She holds in her arms a
"baby of some three months old" which had been born in a "darksome apartment of the prison" (p. 73). In the Overbury materials

14

there also appears an account of the birth of a baby girl to a criminal in prison. Lady Frances was taken in custody in the autumn of 1615, and, in accordance with usual procedure, she awaited her trial in prison. During this interval she gave birth to a daughter. Lady Frances' arraignment was postponed from Michaelmas Term to a little after Easter; "some attributed the cause to bee for that the Countesse was with-child, and in the mean time was delivered of a daughter."[7] Bacon's arraignment speeches indicate that her trial was, in fact, delayed because of "her child-birth."[8] Thus, when she was again able, she was conducted from the Tower to the prisoner's bar to answer to the charge of murdering Overbury. The baby, meanwhile, having been taken from her, Lady Frances appeared at her trial without it.

Hawthorne has Hester keep her baby with her throughout the punishment for its symbolical import. With the "winking baby in her arms" and the ignominious scarlet letter sewed to her bosom, she walks through the marketplace. Coming "to a sort of scaffold, at the western extremity of the market-place," Hester mounts the platform where, according to the sentence, she is to stand for three hours (p. 76). Just above this platform is "a kind of balcony, or open gallery, appended to the meetinghouse." Here sit or stand the tribunal, consisting of the governor, his counselors, a judge, a general, and the ministers. Governor Bellingham has with him "four sergeants about his chair, bearing halberds, as a guard of honor" (pp. 85-86). The description of scenic props and figures concerned in Hester's ordeal on the scaffold closely parallels the description of formalities at Lady Frances' and Carr's trial:

So . . . there being a Seat Royall, placed at the upper end of Westminster-hall, a little short of the Kings Bench, and seats made round about it for the rest of the Justices and Peeres to sit on, and a little Cabin built close by the Common pleas for the Prisoners when they came from the Tower, to bee put to rest them in. . . . [The] Lord High Steward with great state came into Westminster-hall, with his Assistants the Judges, divers Lords and Gentlemen attending, and four Serjeants at Armes before him ascending a little Gallery, made of purpose to keep off the crowd, he takes his seat, and the rest of the Assistants and Peers according to their places. . . . The Prisoners were sent for by the Clerk of the Checquer, whose office it was to attend the Prisoners. . . . [The] Prisoners placed at the Barre, Sir Henry Fanshaw reads the Indictment, to which the Countesse pleaded guilty, and confessed the fact. But Somerset pleaded not guilty.[9]

Minute parallels again emerge. The little balcony or gallery in which the officials sit above Hester coincides with the little gallery in which the Lord High Steward sits. In each description there are four sergeants as honor guards around the most distinguished person. In the *State Trials* these sergeants are said to have maces;[10] the sergeants in the novel have halberds.

Hester Prynne bears her public disgrace with calm dignity. She restrains her impulses to shriek and to cast herself from the scaffold (p. 78). Her composure agrees in some measure with the bearing of Lady Frances at her trial. Bacon said that she showed humility.[11] The letter writer John Chamberlain wrote that she "won pity by her sober demeanor."[12] Yet Lady Frances, and also Anne Turner, did not resist some display of emotion. Anne cried at her trial.[13] At the reading of Lady Frances' arraignment, she "stood, looking pale, trembled, and shed some few tears."[14] But, says Hawthorne, Hester merely "grew pale and trembled" (p. 86).

During her ordeal Hester becomes oblivious to her surroundings. Her active mind summons up pictures of her virtuous youth and stainless maidenhood in England, of her honorable parents, and of her unhappy married life. From the scaffold of the pillory, she traces her life in reverie back along the track "which she had been treading since her happy infancy" (pp. 79, 103). In a similar reminiscing fashion, the ghost of Anne Turner, according to Niccols, reviews her life before the ghost of Overbury. The ghost explains that she had not been base from birth, but that "My nature of itself [was] inclin'd to good." The vanity of court life had led to her downfall. For the benefit of other vain women her ghost continues:

16

Adultery & Ostracism

Observe each step, when first I did begin
To tread the path that led from sin to sin,
Until my most unhappy foot did light,
In guiltless blood of this impoison'd knight.

Her ghost warns others to "mark the path which they do tread."[15]
The shameful recollection of her parents' faces in Hester's reverie
parallels also Lady Frances' thoughts of her mother and father
after she had entered into adultery with Robert Carr. She wrote
to Mrs. Turner that her "Father and Mother are angry" for her
refusal to live with her husband. To Dr. Forman she confided
that she feared the loss of her reputation and that her actions
might carry to her "Father and Mother."[16]

Awaking from her abstraction, Hester gets a view of an elderly
man. Her husband has arrived on the scene. For some time he
has been there, inconspicuously hidden in the throng. Perceiving
that she has noticed him, he beckons her to silence (pp. 81-82).
Chillingworth refuses to come forth to claim her as his wife and
to share in her dishonor. He prefers to remain obscure (p. 145).
Hawthorne's portrayal of the wronged husband at this point has
a parallel in the conduct of Lord Essex. Essex had at first only
mildly reproved his wife, Lady Frances. Later he took her away
from Court to his home at Chartley. But, realizing his situation
was hopeless, he eventually yielded without a contest to her charges
of impotency against him and her divorce. Thereafter he remained out of her life.[17] Further, Andrew Amos writes that "Lord
Essex, the former husband of the Countess, was present at her
trial, but seemed purposely to keep out of public observation and
the sight of the wife of his infancy."[18] Thus, both Essex and Chillingworth, husbands of unfaithful wives, were present at the
moment of their wives' legal sentences, and neither was willing
to be known and share the infamy.

While engaged in thoughts about the wrong she has done to
her husband, Hester hears herself called. John Wilson and Arthur
Dimmesdale seek to elicit from her the name of him who tempted
her to this fall. Hester refuses to make known her companion in

17

adultery. Her obstinacy calls forth an hour's sermon from Wilson (pp. 85-91). This incident of calling Hester's name and of speeches by those sitting in judgment upon her compares with the legal procedure at the trial of Lady Frances. Mr. Fanshaw, the Clerk of the Crown called her name, swore her in, and then read the arraignment against her, to which she pleaded guilty. She was not requested to testify against her lover and husband, Robert Carr. But provision had been made in the event that she should have pleaded not guilty. "There is a direction," wrote Bacon to George Villiers, Duke of Buckingham, "given to Mr. Lieut. by My Lord Chancellor and myself, that . . . Mr. Whiting, the preacher, a discreet Man, and one that was used to Helwisse, should preach before the Lady, and teach her, and move her generally to a clear confession."[19] The *State Trials* includes also a speech that Bacon had prepared to draw forth her confession, if she should have pleaded not guilty.[20] These notions of hesitation to incriminate others and of preaching to a criminal to get a confession stand out for comparison.

Through one of the spectators' remarks to Chillingworth, the reader is informed of the details of Hester's punishment. The townsman states that the magistracy have not enforced the extremity of the law which is death, because of her youth, her beauty, and the possibility of strong temptation in the absence of her husband who may have drowned. "But in their great mercy and tenderness of heart, they have doomed Mistress Prynne to stand only a space of three hours on the platform of the pillory, and then and thereafter, for the remainder of her natural life, to wear a mark of shame upon her bosom" (pp. 83-84). Hawthorne's original plans for a woman adjudged by the Massachusetts law of 1704 are recognizable in Hester's sentence. But prior to this statute the penalty for adultery in New England was death. Lady Frances' sentence for the murder of Sir Thomas Overbury was likewise death: "Thou shalt be carried from hence to the Tower of London, and from thence to the place of execution, where you are to be hanged by the neck till you be dead; and the Lord have mercy upon your soul."[21] But her beauty, her youth, her noble carriage,

18

her submissive confession, her appearance of contrition, and the influence of her family—her father, Thomas Howard, Earl of Suffolk, was Lord Chamberlain; her great-uncle, Henry Howard, Earl of Northampton, was Lord Privy Seal and Lord Warden of the Cinque Ports—combined to gain her clemency. Her sentence contained a clause that this penalty would be subject to revocation if the King could be moved in her behalf. In accordance with this clause, two months after her conviction she received a royal pardon:

This Bill containeth your Majesties gracious Pardon unto the Lady Frances late Countesse of Somerset, for being accessary before the fact, of the Death and Imprisonment of Sir Thomas Overbury. It hath inserted as Motives to your Majesties mercy four respects; that is to say: The respect of her Father, Friends, and Family. Her voluntary Confession, both when she was Prisoner, and at the Barre. The promise made publiquely by the Lord Steward, and her Peers to intercede for your Majesties Mercy: And that the Crime was not of a Principall, but of an Accessary, before the fact, by the instigation of base persons.[22] The like pardon formerly passed your Majesties signature, and is now amended by your Majesties speciall direction from your royall mouth, in two points: the one is, That Imprisonment in the Tower, or other Confining at your Majesties pleasure, is not pardoned; the other, that the solemne Promise made at her Arraignment by the Lord Steward and the Peers to intercede to your Majesty for your Mercy is inserted.[23]

Hester's prison term is likewise not remitted. After her ordeal on the scaffold, she returns to her cell, as Lady Frances was led back to the Tower. The excitement of the preceding three hours strongly affects Hester's passionate nature; by night she grows frenzied and unmanageable. The jailer fears that she may "perpetrate violence on herself, or do some half-frenzied mischief to the poor babe" (p. 92). She explains to Chillingworth that she has had thoughts of death and has even wished for it (p. 95). Lady Frances' conduct offers a parallel to Hester's frenzy. Being warned on Saturday that her trial would begin the following

Wednesday, the Countess "fell that night to casting and scouring, and so continued the next day very sick."[24] Her behavior during this trying period of confinement and pregnancy evoked special care in her attendance lest she kill herself and her baby.[25]

Similarly, Master Brackett, the jailer, ushers in to Hester a newly arrived physician, who for the time is "lodged in the prison, not as suspected of any offence, but as the most convenient and suitable mode of disposing of him, until the magistrates should have conferred with the Indian sagamores respecting his ransom" (pp. 92-93). The prison domicile of Chillingworth and the meeting of husband and wife in jail accord with the facts of the imprisonment of Carr and Lady Frances. After their trials, they were returned to the Tower, and the King desired that the Tower Official "lodge them as neare one to the other as may conveniently be."[26] One source states that "the Earl of Somerset and his lady have the full liberty of the Tower, and converse freely together by day and night."[27]

In the prison interview between Hester and her husband, Hawthorne introduces Chillingworth's sinister scheme of vengeance. Hester is caught in a dilemma. In order to save the man she loves from public disgrace, she is compelled to enter into a bond to conceal her husband's identity. Thus, tacitly she becomes a party to Chillingworth's secret revenge. Chillingworth makes her swear an oath of secrecy: Hester says, "I will keep thy secret, as I have his." But Chillingworth orders her to "Swear it!": "And she took the oath" (p. 99). Hester's oath of secrecy and acquiescence in Chillingworth's scheme of revenge have more than one parallel in the Overbury case. Bacon made the accusation that Carr conspired against Overbury's life out of revenge and that Lady Frances plotted with him: "my Lord of Somerset had made a vow, that Overbury should neither live in Court, nor Country; . . . that either he or himself must die." Thus "divers devices and projects" were "plotted between the Countesse of Essex, and the Earl of Somerset."[28] Bacon also charged that "the purveyance or provisions of the poisons" were brought to Lady Frances "and by her billetted and laid up till they might be used: and this done with an oath or vow of secrecy, which is like the Egyptian darkness, a gross and palpable darkness, that may be felt."[29] After the Countess learned that Weston had revealed her part in the crime, she met with Franklin, "and at that time did again give another oath for secrecy."[30]

An important difference appears between the oath sworn by Hester and the vow of revenge shared by Carr and Lady Frances, as well as the oath given between Lady Frances and Franklin. The Countess is in both instances guilty of a major offense, whereas Hester is a partner only because she is made to pledge her silence. Lady Frances enters fully into the guilt of plotting revenge against Overbury, whereas Hester, because she loves Dimmesdale, thinks that not to reveal his name will protect him from the same black ruin which has overwhelmed her. She is guilty of "acquiescing in Roger Chillingworth's scheme of disguise" (p. 202). Later in the forest she confesses to Dimmesdale that she had striven to be true in all things; "save when thy good,—thy life,—thy fame,— were put in question! Then I consented to a deception" (p. 232). Hester's consent to be silent regarding Chillingworth's identity and plot of revenge, because of her love for Dimmesdale, agrees closely with Niccols' interpretation of Anne Turner's share in Overbury's murder. The poet has Anne's ghost confess to Overbury's ghost these words:

> *Thou gentle knight, whose wrongs I now repent,*
> *Behold a woeful wretch, that did consent*
> *In thy sad death. . . .*
>
> . . . .
>
> *Yet neither thirst of gold, nor hate to thee*
> *For injuries receiv'd, incensed me*
> *To seek thy life; but love, dear love to those*
> *That were my friends, and thy too deadly foes.*[31]

Later in her confession, the ghost is made to explain in more detail her part in the conspiracy:

> *For, when those wantons, whose unjust desire,*
> *Had urg'd me on so far, that to retire*

Part Two — Plot

I knew was vain, as I before to lust
Had been a minister, so now I must
Join hands in blood, which they did plot and study:

. . . .

In mischief I went on, and did agree
To be an actor in thy tragedy,
Thou injur'd ghost; yet was I but a mute,
And what I did was at another's suit:
Their plots I saw, and silent kept the same.[32]

The agreements between Hester's consent to silence and that expressed by Anne's ghost are not exact. Yet, in each instance a woman, by request, consents to be silent regarding a plot on a man's life. Each woman acquiesces because of love, Hester for Dimmesdale, the man plotted against, and Anne for some of the plotters.

Some time later, Hester's term of prison confinement comes to an end. She is released from prison with no restrictive clause that prohibits her from leaving the settlement. Nevertheless, as long as she chooses to remain, she is under the inquisitorial watch of the magistrates. She assumes residence on the outskirts of town, and there in a lonesome dwelling she lives in virtual isolation. Ostracized from society, this pitiable woman seems banished to a solitude as trying as her prison confinement (pp. 101-108).

Hester's isolation resembles that of other Hawthorne characters who for various reasons are cut off from social concourse.[33] Yet Lady Frances also underwent isolation upon her release from the Tower. After her trial, she returned to prison and there remained along with Somerset until their final release six years later, that is, early in 1622. The royal order setting her at liberty provided that she remain confined in the country:

Whereas his Majesty is graciously pleased to enlarge and set at liberty the Earle of Somerset, and his Lady, now Prisoners in the Tower of London; And that neverthelesse it is thought fit, that both the said Earl and his Lady bee confined to some convenient place: It is therefore, according to his Majesties gracious pleasure

22

and command, Ordered, that the Earle of Somerset and his Lady
doe repaire either to Grayes, or Cowsham, the Lord Wallingfords
houses in the County of Oxon, and remain confined to one or either
of the said houses, and within three miles compasse of either of
the same, untill further order be given by his Majesty.[34]

The misery of Lady Frances' life is frequently mentioned. Robert
Codrington, in "The Life and Death of the Illustrious Robert, Earl
of Essex" in *The Harleian Miscellany*, records that the criminals
were "prohibited not to approach the presence of the King, nor
to come within ten miles of his majesty's court. This did beget so
great a discontent, that their love by degrees did begin to suffer
diminution with their pomp."[35] Kempe's account of this phase
of the Countess' life adds to her moral discomfiture a note of
physical misery: "They became indifferent to each other, and
lived apart in obscurity and neglect, the objects of public contempt and execration. She died before her husband, of a decay,
so loathsome, that historians have noticed it as a manifestation
of heaven upon her crimes."[36]

One particular of Hester's banished life is that she frequently
labors in a little garden, where children observe her (pp. 104-105).
Lady Frances also had access to a garden during her prison confinement. Kempe included in his collection of manuscripts a letter
to the Lieutenant of the Tower, George More, from the Council
concerning Lady Frances. "The Countess of Somerset has made
humble suit for a divine to be admitted to her, to afford her
spiritual consolation, and for permission to walk in the garden
adjoining the place of her confinement."[37] Another detail of
Hester's banishment is her nocturnal walks (p. 112). In an early
period of Lady Frances' life, when she was still married to Lord
Essex, she shut herself up, and did not go out except at night.
Kempe narrates that Lord Essex was greatly disappointed to return after three or four years of absence to find his wife's affection
for him estranged. With the assistance of her father, he removed
his wife to his "seat at Chartley, one hundred miles from court.
On her arrival there, she affected to be overcome with a deep
melancholy, refused all society whatever with the Earl, shut her-

self up in her chamber with her female attendants, and stirred out only in the dead of the night."[38] Thus, at two periods of her life, allegedly living in solitude, Lady Frances appears almost a symbol of isolation.

After a lapse of three years, during which time the lonely Hester plies her needle and cares for her little daughter Pearl, she learns that a coterie of the leading inhabitants of the settlement are promoting a scheme to deprive her of her child. They deem her unworthy to provide the elements in the child's education necessary for its soul's salvation. They propose that Pearl be taken from her and be "transferred to wiser and better guardianship than Hester Prynne's" (p. 125). She, therefore, proceeds to Governor Bellingham's mansion to learn the particulars of this plan and to affirm her competence to look after the child's spiritual welfare. To this unhappy woman Governor Bellingham explains that "the point hath been weightily discussed, whether we, that are of authority and influence, do well discharge our consciences by trusting an immortal soul, such as there is in yonder child, to the guidance of one who hath stumbled and fallen, amid the pitfalls of this world" (pp. 136-137).

A contrast to this turn of events occurs in regard to Lady Frances and her baby, who was the daughter not only of an adulteress but also of a murderess with years yet to serve in prison. The infant was taken immediately from her mother's presence, away from the unwholesome environment of the Tower and of a corrupt court, to be brought up in the paths of virtue. Care was taken that she learn nothing of her mother's wicked life. The letter writer Chamberlain gives two pictures of the relationship between mother and daughter. At her incarceration in the Tower, he writes, "the Lady of Somerset was committed . . . upon so short warning that she had scant leisure to shed a few tears over her little daughter at the parting."[39] Some few months later he adds: "The Lady Knollys, and some other friends, have had access to the lady divers times since her conviction, and carried her young daughter to her twice or thrice."[40] The historian Oldmixon writes that the Earl and Countess of Somerset "had one Daughter, who marry'd the Earl, afterwards Duke of Bedford. A Lady as distinguish'd by her Virtue as her Rank; and such Care was taken to conceal from her the odious Character of her Mother, that she had heard nothing of this Story till a Year or two before she dy'd."[41] In contrast, Hawthorne has Hester retain possession of her child.

It is still too early to draw a conclusion, but the agreements between the first unit of the plot of *The Scarlet Letter* and details in the Overbury case challenge the imagination. Lady Frances' adultery and its consequences to her present many parallels with Hester in these early stages of action. A description of Lady Frances' trial and Niccols' picture of a scene at the trials of the accomplices have features that minutely coincide with Hester's punishment upon the scaffold. Lady Frances' trial proceedings present parallels with the events that take place on this day of Hester's shame. Both these women are also guilty of adultery. Both bear a baby girl in prison. Both are returned to prison before they are released. Both undergo a trying ostracism, the one legal, the other moral. Both pledge oaths of secrecy that prepare the way for a deceitful revenge. In each story, the moral welfare of the criminal's child is a matter for some consideration. Regarding the oaths of secrecy, however, Niccols' poetic version of Anne Turner, also an adulteress, offers a parallel more suggestive of the plot of the novel, for, by vowing silence, both Hester and Anne Turner—so Niccols interprets this woman's character—acquiesce in a plot upon a man's life.

❦ 3 ❧

REVENGE & MORAL POISONING

W HILE Hester labors under her doom, her husband, under the name of Roger Chillingworth, assumes a position in the community as a skilful "chirurgeon." In regard to religion his conduct is exemplary. Soon after his arrival he chooses "for his spiritual guide the Reverend Mr. Dimmesdale" (p. 147). In the literature of the Overbury case occurs a relationship with similar characteristics. When Overbury returned from a mission to France, he attracted the attention of Carr, who, now an official secretary and invested with important public responsibility, found in the knight an able adviser. So pleased was Carr with Overbury's diligence and understanding that he took him for his teacher and counselor. According to Bacon, in his prosecution speech at Carr's arraignment, "Sʳ Thomas Overbury for a time was known to have great interest and strait friendship with my Lord of Somerset, both in his meaner fortunes, and after, in so much that he was a kinde of Oracle of direction unto him."[1]

Dimmesdale, whose health has begun to decline, returns the confidence entrusted in him as Chillingworth's spiritual counselor. Submitting to the anxious entreaties of his parishioners, he makes the physician his medical adviser. Mutual trust and respect lead to an intimate friendship. The two men confide in each other many of their secret thoughts. Daily they keep up a "familiar intercourse" (p. 160). They spend much time together in taking walks and in conversing. They discuss not only topics of ethics,

26

of religion, and of other public matters, but they also speak much about matters of a private character, of things "personal to themselves" (p. 153). In the same manner, two intimate friendships developed in the early stages of the Overbury affair. The more prominent is that between Carr and Overbury. Bacon observed that "this friendship rested not only in conversation, and business at Court, but likewise in communication of secrets of State."[2] They "were grown to such inwardness" that they hesitated not to communicate public affairs. On the same relationship, the anonymous narrator wrote that "to the shew of all the world this bond was indissolvible; neither could there bee more friendship used, since there was nothing so secret, nor any matter so private, but . . . [Carr] imparted it to Mr. Overbury."[3]

A second friendship in the Overbury case is one between Carr and Northampton. Noticing Carr's rise and fearing lest the young man would overshadow his own greatness, Northampton—Lady Frances' great-uncle—entered into a bond of friendship with him. By means of Northampton's friendly recognition and praise, "there grows a kind of Community between them, and there wants nothing but entercourse of speech for confirmation of acquaintance, and procuring further relation one to another." At length a great "familiarity growes between them" which concludes in courtly discourses and "constant amity on all hands."[4]

At first, Chillingworth expresses alarm at Dimmesdale's failing health. Gradually the physician begins to perceive that there is an ailment in Dimmesdale's soul. The minister seems to him to be troubled, to be burdened with a spiritual malady. Chillingworth, therefore, strives to lay bare this secret. He scrutinizes the soul of his patient, for "he deemed it essential," writes Hawthorne, "to know the man, before attempting to do him good. Wherever there is a heart and an intellect, the diseases of the physical frame are tinged with the peculiarities of these. In Arthur Dimmesdale, thought and imagination were so active, and sensibility so intense, that the bodily infirmity would be likely to have its groundwork there" (pp. 151-152). Thus Chillingworth delves into Dimmesdale's morbid soul, with both skill and native sagacity, in order

27

to ferret out the burden of his sick heart. A comparable situation is to be found in the annals of the Overbury affair, when, discussing the pomp and outward gaiety of the wedding of Carr and Lady Frances, the narrator writes:

All these things notwithstanding a guilty conscience can never goe without accusation; pensiveness, and sullennesse doe possesse the Earl, his wonted mirth forsakes him, he is cast down, hee takes not that felicity in company he was wont, but still something troubles him: Hereby it is a dangerous thing to fall within the compasse of a guilty conscience, it eateth and consumeth the soule of a man, as rust the iron, or as beating waves the hollow rocks; and though these things are not made publique, yet neverthelesse Northampton observed it in him, and having so admirable a capacity, he could make use of all things; wherefore knowing his disease, viz. his mind seared with a murder, and knowing the Earle tractable as he desired, enters into a familiar discourse with him.[5]

Northampton, who was also guilty of the murder, hoped to salve Carr's conscience to keep him from revealing the secret of the murder, which at this time still had not been brought to light. Chillingworth, in contrast, hopes to discover what secret is affecting Dimmesdale's constitution. In each instance a troubled conscience awakens the interest of a close friend.

Once Chillingworth begins to search Dimmesdale's soul, a terrible fascination gains hold of him. He gives himself up to the search with such diabolical ingenuity that soon he makes a discovery he had hoped for. He becomes aware that the minister is the seducer of his wife. He now alters his course from one of curious investigation to one of deceitful vengeance. Hawthorne observes that "calm, gentle, passionless, as he appeared, there was yet, we fear, a quiet depth of malice, hitherto latent, but active now, in this unfortunate old man, which led him to imagine a more intimate revenge than any mortal had ever wreaked upon an enemy" (p. 170). And he does it by making himself a trusted friend and by taking advantage of this confidence. He still keeps

up his habits of social familiarity, but employs them in the payment of a debt of vengeance.

This motif of revenge upon a trusting friend is a salient feature
in the Overbury murder. Upon learning that Carr and Lady Frances
were planning to marry, Overbury protested vigorously. His interference brought down upon him the wrath of Carr, Lady Frances,
and Northampton. Their friendly regard for him soon turned into
a hate that demanded revenge. They agreed first to remove him
from the country, and Carr, who saw that Overbury was not desirous of an overseas assignment because of his health, urged King
James to appoint him anyway. At the same time, Carr deceitfully
advised Overbury to refuse the post. As Carr foresaw, Overbury
was thrown into prison. Once Overbury was safely away in the
Tower, Carr and Lady Frances proceeded with their marriage
plans. Nevertheless, they agreed that he should be poisoned so
as to cause no interference whatsoever. All this time Carr wrote
to Overbury and promised to intercede on behalf of his release.
He sent him powders which he said were for his health, but which
in reality were poisons. In prison, Overbury supposed that "all
was done out of faith and honesty."[6] But at Carr's arraignment,
Bacon pronounced this relationship to be "murther under the
colour of friendship."[7] He characterized Carr's conduct as an excess
of friendship which ended in mortal hatred. Carr's action reflected,
Bacon further charged, a "deep malice, mixed with fear, and not
only matter of revenge upon his Lordship's quarrel."[8] Carr's treatment of Overbury thus epitomizes betrayed confidence and friendship turned to malicious revenge.

Dimmesdale's health (to return to the novel) fails steadily. He
grows gradually more infirm from a mysterious disease. His body,
and with it his life, seems to waste away. His emaciated frame
throbs with the tortures of physical and moral pain. His parishioners, who attribute his decline to excessive study, are certain that
he has not long to live (pp. 147-149). In order to care more closely
for his health, Chillingworth arranges that the two of them may
be lodged together. The physician looks after Dimmesdale's diet,
as well as his lodgings (p. 153). He brings to bear all his skill as

29

a doctor of physic in the treatment of Dimmesdale's illness (pp. 165-167). Similarly, Overbury suffered a decline in health. He gave failing health as his reason for refusing the diplomatic assignment. At Weston's trial, one of Overbury's servants testified that, prior to his prison confinement, Overbury was in fair health; he had merely a complaint from the spleen, caused by "continuall sitting at his study."[9] Yet in prison, after being given poisons, he grew more ill. By means of these poisons, writes the narrator, Overbury "begins to grow extream sickly, having been heretofore accustomed to very good health, in so much as he can scarce stand or goe, what with the pain of his body, and the heat."[10] Overbury was poisoned over a period of five months with a variety of poisons and methods of administering them. His murderers conspired to bring about a slow death in order not to arouse suspicion of foul play. Franklin was hired to provide a poison "which should not kill a man presently, but lie in his body for a certain time, wherewith he might languish away by little and little."[11] Under such treatment, Overbury passed his "tedious and sorrowfull daies . . . with paines and grief"; he wasted away unnaturally "as a man in a Consumption, but with much more extremity."[12] Niccols has the ghost of Overbury describe this painful mode of death, including the element of deception, in his "Vision":

> *Month after month, they often did instill*
> *The divers natures of that baneful ill,*
> *Throughout these limbs: inducing me to think,*
> *That what I took in physick, meat, or drink,*
> *Was to restore me to my health; when all*
> *Was but with ling'ring death to work my fall.*[13]

The connection between Chillingworth's revenge upon Dimmesdale and the latter's languishing sickness is not made perfectly clear. Chillingworth seems to be caring for the minister's health with all the pharmaceutical knowledge available in his day. He is seen gathering weeds in the forest. Dimmesdale observes him in his laboratory where he converts these weeds into potent drugs (p. 160). Yet the people begin to feel a prejudice towards this man of science. Some of them believe him to be versed in the miraculous cures of the black art (p. 156). Others, believing him to be a potent necromancer, suspect him of giving poisonous drugs to their minister (p. 305). They have no proof, but there circulates a story that Chillingworth had been seen "at the period of Sir Thomas Overbury's murder." One citizen "testified to having seen the physician, under some other name, which the narrator of the story had now forgotten, in company with Doctor Forman, the famous old conjurer, who was implicated in the affair of Overbury" (pp. 155-156).

Hawthorne's allusion to Overbury's murder at this stage of the novel not only strengthens the validity of the previous parallels, but also provides an explicit comparison between the plot on that man's life and the vengeful plot of Chillingworth on Dimmesdale. It has already been noticed that the unlawful love of Carr and Lady Frances, their oaths of revenge against Overbury, and the course of Carr's friendship parallel the broad development of the story of *The Scarlet Letter*. Now, in the insinuations that Chillingworth may be poisoning Dimmesdale, as Overbury was poisoned, there emerges a closer parallel, and it is drawn by Hawthorne himself. Franklin, for instance, "a kind of Physitian," was employed to make poisons, "for hee was excellent in that art."[14] Niccols has the ghost of Franklin say to the ghost of Overbury that "I was the man/ That did prepare those poisons, which began/ And ended all thy pain."[15] Chillingworth's compounding of drugs is thus comparable to the poisonous art of the murderers of Overbury, and especially of Franklin, a physician, a man skilled in the arts of poisoning, and—as will later appear—like Chillingworth, a man with a crooked shoulder. There is, however, this notable difference between the poisoning of Overbury and Chillingworth's compounding of poisonous drugs to use on the minister: the former was actually a poisoning, but it is merely rumored that Chillingworth is poisoning Dimmesdale. The real poisoning of Dimmesdale seems to lie elsewhere.

But first, two other items for comparison appear in this reference to Overbury. Both relate to Chillingworth. One concerns his becoming a medical adviser to Dimmesdale; the other concerns the means whereby Chillingworth is paying his debt of vengeance. The friendship between Carr and Overbury, it has been shown, agrees with that between Dimmesdale and Chillingworth, though not in every respect. Overbury was the counselor or the oracle of direction to Carr, and Dimmesdale is the spiritual guide of Chillingworth. But there was no clear parallel for Chillingworth as medical adviser to Dimmesdale. In Carr's pretended concern for Overbury's health, as illustrated by his sending powders to the prisoner, this element faintly appears, but the fact that Franklin was a psysician and was employed in the preparation of poisons completes the parallel of professional advice. While Overbury's oracular relation to Carr agrees with Dimmesdale's similar relation to Chillingworth, Franklin's capacity as a physician hired to poison Overbury contrasts with Chillingworth's medical supervision of Dimmesdale's health. There were also some physicians who visited Overbury in prison and seemed honestly to try to restore him to health. Overbury himself, growing suspicious of his attendant Weston, once asked for a physician.[16]

Still, in this allusion to Overbury occurs a parallel to another means, besides rumored poisoning, whereby Chillingworth is gaining revenge on Dimmesdale. Hawthorne suggests that the physician is tormenting Dimmesdale's conscience with conjured spirits. Chillingworth becomes "not a spectator only, but a chief actor in the poor minister's interior world. . . . The victim was forever on the rack; it needed only to know the spring that controlled the engine; and the physician knew it well! Would he startle him with sudden fear? As at the waving of a magician's wand, uprose a grisly phantom,—uprose a thousand phantoms,—in many shapes, of death, or more awful shame, all flocking round about the clergyman, and pointing with their fingers at his breast!" (p. 171). This fantastic motif also occurs elsewhere in the novel. Chillingworth has reportedly associated with the conjurer Forman and has participated in Indian incantations (pp. 155-156). And some people believe him to be a potent necromancer (p. 305).

Both Forman and Franklin—with the latter of whom Hawthorne

may be comparing Chillingworth in the allusion—were conjurers. When Lady Frances first fell in love with Robert Carr, she went to Anne Turner for help. They decided to enchant Carr: "For this purpose they fall acquainted with Dr. Forman that dwelt at Lambeth, being an ancient Gentleman, was thought to have skill in the Magick Art."[17] Until his death, Forman helped them devise means of witchcraft to induce love in Carr. Later, Gresham and finally Franklin were hired for these evil purposes. Franklin was "thought to bee no lesse a witch then the two former, Forman and Gresham."[18] In "Sir Thomas Overbury's Vision," Richard Niccols has the ghost of Franklin say that "Forman, that cunning exorcist, and I/ Would many times our wicked wits apply/ Kind nature" in conjuring spirits.[19]

The question still remains whether Dimmesdale, as Overbury was, is being poisoned to death. In a metaphorical sense Hester thinks he is: "She doubted not, that the continual presence of Roger Chillingworth,—the secret poison of his malignity, infecting all the air about him,—and his authorized interference, as a physician, with the minister's physical and spiritual infirmities,—that these bad opportunities had been turned to a cruel purpose. By means of them, the sufferer's conscience had been kept in an irritated state" (p. 231). In another place, Hawthorne observes that it was impossible for her to doubt "that, whatever painful efficacy there might be in the secret sting of remorse" in the minister's conscience, "a deadlier venom had been infused into it by the hand that proffered relief. A secret enemy had been continually by his side, under the semblance of a friend and helper" (p. 201). In terms crudely similar, the ghost of Overbury is made to say to Niccols in the "Vision" that he had served a false friend and that cruel men had vengefully induced him to take food containing poisons. Slowly this "poison secretly did creep/ Through" his veins. "The venom, seizing" him "vulture-like," painfully tore his entrails.[20] In the Overbury case, however, the poisons were chemical; in Chillingworth's revenge, the poisoning is what Bacon called a "circumstance moral," in that it is revenge upon a trusting friend.[21] For Hawthorne implies that Dimmesdale is poisoned by breathing a moral atmosphere polluted with the venom of Chillingworth's secret malignity.

The contrasts between the two poisonings may be carried still further. Dimmesdale is also poisoned by a guilty conscience. Hawthorne writes that "the poison of one morbid spot was infecting his heart's entire substance" (p. 172). His sin and the failure to confess it ulcerate his moral system. His guilty conscience festers and generates an infectious poison that spreads fatally throughout his nature. His spirit becomes sick; his heart grows morbid. Dimmesdale's languishing sickness, because of the poisoning of his system, parallels Overbury's consumptive decay from the poisons administered him. But in the Overbury case there are two men guilty of sin who, like Dimmesdale, suffered in their consciences. Carr's guilty conscience and diseased mind have been observed. But Jervase Helwyse' situation is more germane. Helwyse was guilty of conniving in the plot on Overbury's life. As Lieutenant of the Tower, he had known about the murder, but had remained silent. How far he was involved in the crime is not certain. But it is clear that his conscience bothered him. His ghost is made by Niccols to confess to the ghost of Overbury that "of no sin had my most sinful soul/ Been ever sick, [but] . . . this one sin most foul."[22]

Dimmesdale fights a losing battle with his Puritan conscience. A moral conflict between the forces of confession and secrecy rages within his breast. "Remorse" incites him to confession, while "Cowardice" restrains him (p. 180). Chillingworth urges him to confess the sin that is causing his strange malady, but Dimmesdale replies that he fears to show his spotted soul before his parishioners, lest he lose their respect and the capacity to achieve further religious good (pp. 160-163). Dimmesdale's moral cowardice and the arguments in his conflict are analogous with the problems confronting Helwyse, as expressed by his ghost in Niccols' poem; the ghost confesses his connivance in the murder and explains that his "coward conscience" forced him to yield to secrecy:

Revenge & Moral Poisoning

O what a tedious combate, in my heart,
Unto my soul did feelingly appear,
'Twixt my sad conscience, and a doubtful fear!
Fear said that, if I did reveal the same,
Those great ones, great in grace, would turn the shame
Upon my head; but conscience said again,
That, if I did conceal it, murder's stain
Would spot my soul as much for my consent,
As if at first it had been my intent.
Fear said that, if the same I did disclose,
The countenance of greatness I should lose,
And be thrust out of office and place;
But conscience said that I should lose that grace
And favour, which my God to me had given,
And be perhaps thrust ever out of heaven.
Long these two champions did maintain the field,
Till my weak conscience at the last did yield.

. . . .

Let such men to remember still be mov'd,
That which by sad experience I have prov'd;
'Tis good to fear great men, but yet 'tis better
Ever to fear God more, since God is greater.[23]

The situations agree in that each involves a man with a guilty conscience. In each, a cowardly conscience constrains a sinner to silence. There is a conflict between courting the respect of men and conducting one's self truthfully before God. In *The Scarlet Letter,* the moral conflict is introduced partly through dialogue; Chillingworth, ironically, represents conscience and truth.

Dimmesdale augments his intense pain by performing acts of penance. In an effort to expiate his crime he scourges his soul and keeps nightly vigils. On one of these occasions he walks to the scaffold where Hester had seven years before been condemned to stand. Here by coincidence he meets Hester and Pearl, who are returning from the deathbed of Governor Winthrop. The three join hands. Dimmesdale reinforces the mockery of repentance by declining Pearl's invitation to stand there the following day before the populace; and, as if in reply, there gleams a meteoric light far across the sky. Hawthorne writes that "the great vault brightened, like the dome of an immense lamp." And there in the zenith appears "an immense letter,—the letter A,—marked out in lines of dull red light" (pp. 187, 189).

In the Overbury case occurred a nighttime scaffold scene with details similar to this one in the novel. Robert Carr's trial extended from morning until late in the evening, so long that it was necessary to light Westminster Hall. Andrew Amos describes the trial thus: "The Earl's trial lasted from nine in the morning till ten at night. Towards the concluding part of the trial, the dramatic effect of the scene was increased by a multitude of torches casting a glimmering light through the high and vaulted roofs of the Hall, and making transiently visible the countenances of the Judges, the Counsellors, the Peers, Peeresses, and the mixed audience that crowded the lofty scaffoldings."[24] Striking similarities emerge. In both scenes a guilty man is, as it were, standing on trial—Carr before a legal tribunal, Dimmesdale before a divine tribunal. A dramatic effect arises from a play of lights. At first, Dimmesdale's surroundings are lighted by Wilson's lantern, which casts a "glimmering light," and then by a meteor. When the light from the meteor flashes, "the great vault" of the sky, like the "vaulted roofs of the Hall," is brightened. And just as the torches in the Hall at Carr's trial outlined indistinctly the personages, the light of heaven gave a distinctness to the scene in Boston, but "with the awfulness that is always imparted to familiar objects by an unaccustomed light. . . . all were visible, but with a singularity of aspect that seemed to give another moral interpretation to the things of this world than they had ever borne before" (p. 187).

The midnight vigil, which brings Hester and Dimmesdale together, enables Hester to make the startling discovery that Dimmesdale is on the verge of lunacy. Her vow of secrecy comes squarely home to her, for she realizes that she is largely to blame for the minister's decay. Hester thus determines "to redeem her error, so far as it might yet be possible." Acting upon this resolution, she decides to take the first opportunity to accost Chillingworth and learn what lies yet "in her power for the rescue of the victim on whom he had so evidently set his gripe" (pp. 201-202). Meeting him, she explains that she can no longer hold her silence; she "must reveal the secret" (p. 209). The reports of the Overbury trials include a statement by one of the plotters that he had wanted to back out of the intrigue. Franklin, with whom Lady Frances had made an oath of secrecy, reported to Lord Chief Justice Coke: "I went to her and told her I was weary of it; and I besought her upon my knees, that she would use mee no more in those matters."[25] However, there seems to exist no record that Lady Frances renounced her vow of vengeance, although one of the reasons publicly given for King James's pardon of her, that her complicity in the crime was not premeditated but was forced upon her "by the instigation of base persons" (above, p. 19), does suggest the line Hawthorne follows. But in Niccols' version of Anne Turner's part in the crime there appears a more vivid analogy to Hester's renunciation of her oath. Anne's ghost is made to repent her agreement in life to silence about the murder. Her ghost's confession to the ghost of the man she had wronged is prefaced by a declaration of repentance and is concluded by a request for mercy: "Thou gentle knight, whose wrongs I now repent,/ Behold a woeful wretch, that did consent/ In thy sad death," she begins; she ends with "forget my great offence,/ Which I have purg'd with tears of penitence."[26]

Strangely enough, in introducing the forest interview, during which Hester explains her having "consented" to the plot on Dimmesdale's life, Hawthorne presents his two characters as ghosts. When she first meets him, they question each other's bodily existence. "It was no wonder," writes Hawthorne. "So strangely did they meet, in the dim wood, that it was like the first encounter, in the world beyond the grave, of two spirits who had been intimately connected in their former life, but now stood coldly shuddering, in mutual dread; as not yet familiar with their state, nor wonted to the companionship of disembodied beings. Each a ghost, and awe-stricken at the other ghost!" (Pp. 227-228.) Although Hester wishes she did not have "this grievous wrong to

37

confess" to him she loves, she nevertheless tells him of her error. She confesses that she "consented to a deception" in order to save him. She reveals Chillingworth's identity and implores forgiveness for keeping it a secret (p. 232). Thus in the novel, as in the poem, a woman who has agreed to acquiesce in a plot that wrongs a man's life confesses her guilt and begs forgiveness. In both works, the characters concerned are presented as ghosts.

One other detail of the forest interview seems comparable with elements in the Overbury case. Arthur Dimmesdale and Hester Prynne having agreed to elope, Hester discards her scarlet letter. Undoing her cap, she lets down her hair, which falls "upon her shoulders, dark and rich, with at once a shadow and a light in its abundance, and imparting the charm of softness to her features. . . . Her sex, her youth, and the whole richness of her beauty, came back from what men call the irrevocable past, and clustered themselves, with her maiden hope, and a happiness before unknown, within the magic circle of this hour" (p. 243). Hester's releasing of her hair and her maiden hope for happiness recall a prominent detail in Lady Frances' divorce proceedings and her wedding to Robert Carr. Earlier she had given love phials to Carr, but she had also given drugs to Essex to produce frigidity in him. When her witchcraft upon her unsuspecting husband appeared to succeed, she hastened to report his insufficiency and her virginity. Announcing that she was still a maid, she requested a divorce. Because the Earl of Essex, her husband, was "unable (as she reported) to execute the office of a husband, and that upon search, by the verdict of twelve Matrons shee appeared still to be a Maid," it was decreed that she be granted a divorce, for procreation's sake.[27] At her wedding, Lady Frances kept up the ruse. She created quite an impression at the ceremony, because she came bedecked not as a widow but as a maiden. She appeared "in the habit of a virgin bride," writes Kempe, "her beautiful tresses flowing over her shoulders to her feet."[28] The incident also attracted the attention of Chamberlain, who wrote to a friend, "She was married in her hair."[29] Commenting on this phrase, Amos explains further that "to be married 'in their hair' was the appropriate etiquette of that day for virgin-brides."[30] Quite different is Lady Frances' situation at the Court of King James and that of Hester in the forest. Lady Frances claimed virginity; Hester does not. Lady Frances obtained a divorce and married her lover; Hester seeks no divorce, but plans to elope with Dimmesdale to a foreign country. Yet in each case there are similarities. Each adulteress is shown arrayed in long hair at a scene dealing with her marriage or with her plans to elope. The authors describing these scenes point out a symbolic connection between the long hair and maidenhood. Whereas Kempe makes this connection explicitly, Hawthorne merely implies that Hester's releasing of her long hair symbolizes her hope for future marital happiness, long denied her, and that this hope has a maidenly sincerity about it.

Parallels between the novel and the Overbury affair have thus continued to accumulate, some immediately convincing, others more remote, but altogether forming a pattern that seems to reveal a creative mind at work selecting and rearranging. In this chapter, the essential features of the actual murder of Overbury have been shown to compare with Chillingworth's vengeful plot against Dimmesdale. Both intrigues are marked by a close friendship, and in each instance this friendship turns to deceitful revenge. Both plots are characterized by failing health; in each case poisoning appears as a decisive factor in this languishing death, for Dimmesdale's parishioners voice their fear of a poisonous plot on their minister like that which befell Overbury. In each instance a guilty conscience for concealment of sin is a prominent feature; but the novel, in contrast, tightly integrates into one relationship elements of friendship, revenge, poisoning, guilt, and languishing death; whereas in the Overbury affair these elements are scattered loosely among several relationships. And finally, Hester's symbolic releasing of her hair as she looks forward to an unknown happiness by eloping with her lover vaguely parallels Lady Frances' false declaration of virginity and her maidenly dress at her marriage with her paramour. Are there further parallels in the outcomes of these two stories?

ᑲᔆᐎᔆ 4 ᔆᐎᔆᓭ

FINAL CONFESSION & DEATH

Before Hester and Dimmesdale can embark for their appointed place of escape, the minister, as was decided at the forest interview, goes through with plans to deliver the Election Sermon, a privilege he had long looked forward to. The awaited day having arrived, Dimmesdale preaches the most eloquent sermon in his career. With the congregation he then marches to the town hall to attend the annual banquet in honor of the newly elected magistrates. But weakened by his strange malady and exhausted by his efforts in the pulpit, he totters nervelessly in the ranks of the procession; he can scarcely make his way, but still he shrugs off the assistance of the Reverend John Wilson. As he passes the scaffold, he finally pauses, calls to Hester and Pearl, and then approaches to ascend its steps (p. 300). Unable any longer to conceal his guilt, and fearful lest he die before confessing it, he reveals to the people the secret of his sin with Hester. He stands out distinctly, Hawthorne writes, as he puts "in his plea of guilty at the bar of Eternal Justice." He addresses the "dignified and venerable rulers," his brother ministers, and the "people, whose great heart was thoroughly appalled," and discloses how he had concealed his sin and become "the one sinner of the world." He explains that God knew his guilt. He observes that it was God's will that he has been led to this scaffold, and that he must "do the will which He hath made plain" before his sight (p. 301).

This vivid picture of Dimmesdale's declaration of guilt just before his death has a parallel in the confession speech of Jervase Helwyse before this condemned man's execution. Helwyse, it will be remembered, has been compared to Dimmesdale. Both men were guilty of concealing a sin, and both suffered in their consciences. Just as Dimmesdale, marching in file, stops at the scaffold and ascends it, Helwyse proceeded to the scaffold and mounted it to be executed:

On Monday, 20 Novemb. 1615. hee was executed at Tower-hill upon a Gibbet there set of purpose, about six of the clock in the morning, hee being arrayed in a black Suit, and black Jerkin. . . . He came on foot to the Gibbet from Sheriff Goare's house, between Dr. Whyting, and Dr. Felton, two of his Majesties Chaplains, and coming to the Ladders foot, he talked a word or two to the Executioner. Then he went up the Ladder four or five steps . . . whereafter a while sitting easily, he uttered words to this, or the like effect."[1]

Then Helwyse, like Dimmesdale, addresses the people, confesses his guilt, acknowledges his concealment of a crime, and puts in his plea of guilty, not before a legal tribunal—which has already sentenced him—but before a divine tribunal:

Nobles, right worshipfull, and others, I am here come, as well to shew, explain, & unfold that which at the time of my arraignm. so many of you as were present expected; as also to shew that then I perceived I had lost the good opinion of many, in standing so long upon my innocency, which was my fault, I confesse, hoping now to recover the same, and your good charitable opinions of me, which fault I then saw not, being blinded with mine errors, which made me accompt it no sin. But since my Condemnation, by means and help of these two Gentlemen here present, (the two Doctors) I was perswaded of the greatnesse of my sin, and that it was so much the greater, by how much the more I did conceal it; which by Gods mercy I perceiving, consulted not with flesh and blood, but thought in this my Condemnation, my best way for my souls health to reveale to the omnipotent and all-seeing God, the most secret and inward intentions and thoughts of my deceitfull heart, not once respecting the pains or dispraises of the world, which I regard not at all. . . . Some here knew my forwardnesse . . . but

I plead not innocency that way, but cast it off, and confesse, that of this great assembly I am the most Wretched sinner.[2]

Thus, in the same spirit as Dimmesdale, Helwyse confesses to having hidden his guilt, hastens to make right his accounts with God before his death, and claims to be the worst of sinners for his criminal conduct.

After his speech, Dimmesdale sinks down. In his last words to Hester he expresses his assurance of salvation. He knows God has been merciful to him and has saved him because of the way in which God has tormented him and brought him to death in this fashion:

The law we broke!—the sin here so awfully revealed!—let these alone be in thy thoughts! I fear! I fear! It may be that, when we forgot our God,—when we violated our reverence each for the other's soul,—it was thenceforth vain to hope that we could meet hereafter, in an everlasting and pure reunion. God knows; and He is merciful! He hath proved his mercy, most of all, in my afflictions. By giving me this burning torture to bear upon my breast! By sending yonder dark and terrible old man, to keep the torture always at red-heat! By bringing me hither, to die this death of triumphant ignominy before the people! Had either of these agonies been wanting, I had been lost forever! Praised be his name! His will be done! Farewell! (P. 304.)

Helwyse, likewise, experiences the assurance of salvation in his confession speech. He, too, feels that God has shown him mercy by arranging events so that he can die a death, though perhaps ignominious to some, yet to him a special favor:

Nobles and others, to see your faces it rejoiceth me, whereby you manifest your love in granting my request, to be Witnesses of my Death, I see a number of my friends, there, there, there, pointing as he spake, who out of their loves, I entreated to beseech God to strengthen me in Death, though ignominious to some, yet to mee a bitter cup mingled to me with Gods mercy, a speciall favour this way to call mee home, whereas hee might have taken away my life by shooting the Bridge, or some fall or otherwise; and then this unrepented sin, which I accounted no sin (such was my blind-

42

nesse) had been damnation to mee, for God is just, and the un-repenting sinner shall have no salvation. There is none of you present here that knows how or in what sort hee shall die, it may bee in his bed, it may be otherwise, (God knows); I protest before you all, I never came over this Hill in the chiefest of all my prosperity, with more joy then now I have at this present, for I now know that presently I shall behold the glorious face and sight of my Creator.[3]

In his final prayer Helwyse, like Dimmesdale, reiterates his assurance that he is not lost: "this comfort, this I have, that I am thine; for were I not thine, then out of the root of me could not the buds of repentance appear, by wch I know thou lovest me; it is not I, but thou Lord hast drawne me to thee, for thine own mercies sake, on which mercy, and thy promises made to the true repentant sinner, once again I rely."[4]

Dying speeches of criminals tend to run in familiar patterns. Yet there are more outstanding similarities in Helwyse's confession and in Dimmesdale's dying revelation of his guilt than seems normal. One of these has not been observed. Neither Dimmesdale nor Helwyse states explicitly what sin he has hidden. So ambiguously does Dimmesdale speak of his guilt that some parishioners do not hear in his dying words even a remote implication of his sinning with Hester. Similarly, Helwyse did not mention the crime of murder for which he was about to lose his life. The emphasis in each scene is on having concealed a sin, on a humanly ignominious but divinely merciful death in which the will of God has seemed to prevail, and finally on the experience of the assurance of salvation.

At Chillingworth's death, which follows hard upon Dimmesdale's, "he bequeathed a very considerable amount of property, both here and in England, to little Pearl, the daughter of Hester Prynne" (p. 308). Pearl became the richest heiress in New England. In the Overbury affair, Anne Carr, the daughter born to Lady Frances in prison, was similarly provided for. Before her father, Robert Carr, went on trial for the murder of Overbury, he wrote to King James a declaration of his innocence and at the same time requested permission from the King to "dispose of my lands and goods to my wife and child."[5] This detail occurs also in Carr's later petition to King Charles I for reinstatement into royal favor.[6] Chillingworth, in contrast, is not actually Pearl's father, nor does he bequeath anything to Hester, his wife.

Rumors later circulate that Pearl becomes a bride and that she gives birth to a baby. She and her mother had left their peninsula cottage, and years later Hester returns alone. "But, through the remainder of Hester's life, there were indications that the recluse of the scarlet letter was the object of love and interest with some inhabitant of another land. Letters came, with armorial seals upon them, though of bearings unknown to English heraldry" (pp. 309-310). The gossips believe that Pearl is "not only alive, but married, and happy, and mindful of her mother." Hester is said to be making baby garments, presumably for Pearl's infant (p. 310). Pearl's noble marriage and her giving birth to a child are also analogous with facts in the career of Anne Carr. Married in 1637 to William Russell, Duke of Bedford, Anne Carr gave birth to at least one child.[7] Whereas Anne Carr, however, married into the English nobility, Pearl appears to have married into a peerage other than English.

Hester herself lives out her life in lonely sorrow. Her troubles draw many women to her for consultation and advice on marital problems. The circumstances attending the death of Lady Frances are hardly a close parallel. Hester dies later than her husband, but Lady Frances preceded her husband in death: she died in 1632, and he in 1645. Hester becomes the object of much honorable respect before she dies, but Lady Frances is said to have died in obscurity.[8] Though indelibly stained with sin, Hester, moreover dies a serene death, but Lady Frances, the "fatal countesse," died from a revoltingly loathsome disease.[9] *The Biographia Britannica* records that the Countess "yet underwent a much more miserable fate in her death, occasioned by a gangrene that ended in a mortification of that part, in which she had almost beyond all example shamelessly offended." For " 'tis said she had a procidentia vulvae & uteri, which hanging down inverted to her knees, and mortifying

44

piecemeal, caused the most excruciating tortures."[10] By sharp contrast, the woman who has paralleled Hester in so many aspects of her career dies a death shockingly repulsive. Hawthorne places the emphasis in Hester's death rather on the pollution of her soul which denies her all opportunity of fulfilling a divine mission for improving the status of woman; this inability, Hawthorne implies, is a divine judgment for her sin (p. 311). But the details of Lady Frances' death concern her bodily pollution, which is also attributed to the judgment of God upon her.[11]

Any one of the parallels that have been drawn, thus far, may have occurred to Hawthorne independently of influence from the Overbury affair: adultery, a prison birth of a baby girl, a legal proceeding, a prison interview between husband and wife, a vow of revenge made by a husband in which a faithless wife acquiesces for her own reasons, virtual ostracism from society; a close friendship, a deceitful revenge upon a trusting friend, a guilty conscience, a languishing sickness with intimations of poisoning, a nightly scaffold scene, the repenting of having made an oath by a woman who consented to silence, a hope for happiness by joining with a paramour; a dying confession made by a man who has concealed his guilt, an experience at death of the blessed assurance of divine mercy and salvation, a bequeathing of property to a daughter, and a noble marriage of a young girl. Any one of these elements, to repeat, or even a number of them, may have been suggested to Hawthorne from various and sundry places. But such a chain of agreements, as this one, demands some kind of explanation other than coincidence. Since these parallels are all found in literary documents relating to a single episode in history, there is a strong degree of probability that they may have been the imaginative materials that inspired Hawthorne to complete in novel form the idea for a tale of adultery that had lain dormant in his mind for many years.

The unity of the elements that parallel the design of the novel also argues for a probable influence. The first unit of the plot, up to the scene at Bellingham's mansion, concerns, for the most part, Hester—her prison term for adultery, her punishment, and her thoughts in her banished condition. The parallels to this section of the novel group themselves around the corresponding prison term for murder, the trial, the release, and the banishment of Lady Frances, an adulteress. Similarly, when the author shifts, after the scene at Bellingham's mansion, to the relationship between Chillingworth and Dimmesdale, the parallels to the action in these chapters—friendship, revenge, and poisoning of Dimmesdale's system—are clustered about the Carr-Overbury friendship which ended in the poisonous murder of Overbury instigated by the vengeful Carr. And in the same fashion, the parallels to the catastrophe of the novel, that is, Dimmesdale's revelatory speech before his death, center in the confession of Helwyse before his execution.

Nor is it insignificant that in "The Custom House" Hawthorne mentioned, perhaps facetiously, that he adapted the main facts of the novel from an existing story and vouched for "the authenticity of the outline" (pp. 51-52). The outline of the Overbury murder consists initially of adultery between Lady Frances and Robert Carr. Their love precipitated the vengeful murder of Overbury, who had opposed their marriage. The plot concludes with the confessions and punishment of the criminals. In spite of the totally different array of characters and of emotional effect, the outline of action in the novel fundamentally agrees. Hester's adultery leads to Chillingworth's revenge, and at the end Dimmesdale confesses his guilt. But, in sharp contrast, the novel possesses a degree of artistic unity lacking in full accounts of the Overbury murder. The motifs that in the murder are loose and scattered are amalgamated in a few characters in the novel.

The inherent probability that the Overbury affair became transmuted into *The Scarlet Letter* is greater in view of Hawthorne's citations of Overbury in the novel. But the theory also merits consideration in the light of Hawthorne's interests and predilections. His mind had perhaps been working unconsciously, as it were, on the idea of a tale of adultery, and it was, therefore, drawn towards this salient motif in the Overbury crime. He may also have been attracted to the case, as has been mentioned, by the recurrence of the name Jervase Helwyse in both his family tree and in the

Overbury case; at any rate, he had used the name in 1838 in "Lady Eleanor's Mantle." Many times earlier, Hawthorne had written tales which used sin as a basis; more than once before he had dealt with hidden sin and a guilty conscience. Obsessed artistically with moral issues, his temperament could have found it congenial to assimilate the Overbury materials because of their preoccupation with sin, guilt, and judgment upon the sinner. All the evidence, however, is still not in. May there not be further elements in the case that parallel the distinctive features of the characters, the setting, and the style of the novel—coincidences which may further strengthen this hypothesis?

ᐸᒍᐳᔿ 5 ᔿᐸᒍᐳ

HESTER PRYNNE

IN ACCORDANCE WITH Hawthorne's usual method of forming characters by combining details from several different persons,[1] traits of Hester Prynne parallel features of both Lady Frances and Anne Turner. Guilty of adultery like Hester, these two participants in the murder of Overbury have also been seen to resemble her at many other stages in the plot of the novel. While in prison awaiting their sentences, Hester and Lady Frances each bears a baby daughter. Each gives an oath of secrecy in a plot of revenge, undergoes ostracism following her prison term, and employs the symbolic guise of a virgin in connection with a new union. Hester and Anne Turner analogously acquiesce in a plot of revenge. And each is shown repenting of her consent to secrecy and obtaining forgiveness from the avenged man. There are also a few other comparisons to be drawn between Hester and these two women.

One of Hester's most distinctive traits is her skill at needlework. Her fine art of sewing brings her a small reputation. The matronly judges have only contempt for her needlework, but by this art Hester occupies herself both during her prison confinement and throughout her lengthy isolation. She makes her own dresses and those of Pearl. She supplies the vain members of the community with "deep ruffs, painfully wrought bands, and gorgeously embroidered gloves" (p. 105). Because of this superior "gift for devising drapery and costume" (p. 214), her handiwork sets the fashion of the age (p. 106).

The vocation of Anne Turner coincides with that of Hester. Listed among other items in an inventory of Anne Turner's personal belongings, confiscated by the court at her execution, is a set of needlework pearls. Most of the other possessions are clothes: "An ashcoloured sattin nightgown; another of changeable taffata; a black taffata strait-bodiced gown; others of sattin, wattered sattin, etc.; a black shag nightgown; an old taffata petticoat; three waistcoats; a gown of wrought grogram; six smocks; two laced aprons; a square of needlework pearls."[2] As Hester makes fashionable ruffs and bands, so also Anne Turner made ruffs and cuffs and introduced fashions of dress into courtly circles. The starched yellow ruff is said to have been her invention. Robert Codrington, in his life of Essex included in *The Harleian Miscellany*, writes that Mistress Turner "is the woman who first invented, and brought into fashion the use of yellow starch."[3] Richard Niccols has the ghost of Anne express contempt for this vain, colorful creation: "pride," says her ghost,

> *Taught me each fashion, brought me over seas*
> *Each new device, the humorous time to please:*
> *But of all vain inventions, then in use*
> *When I did live, none suffer'd more abuse*
> *Than that fantastick ugly fall and ruff,*
> *Daub'd o'er with that base starch of yellow stuff.*[4]

Thus Hester and Anne each possesses a skill at needlework, each makes ruffs, and each sets fashions.

With her talent, Hester embroiders the scarlet letter which she has been sentenced to wear for a time on the scaffold and thereafter for life (p. 84). The letter is the "badge" of her shame (pp. 137, 197, 204, 305). The fate of Anne Turner is remarkably similar. She too was sentenced to a shameful punishment on the scaffold at which time she had to wear the product of her own fancy, the yellow starched ruffs and cuffs. In the introduction to *The Narrative History*, Michael Sparke observes that Lord Chief Justice Edward Coke sentenced "that fomenter of Lust, Mistris Anne Turner . . . to be hanged at Tiburn in her yellow Tiffiny Ruff and Cuffs, being she was the first Inventer and wearer of that horrid Garb"; and such an impression this rare sight of the hanging of a gaily starched witch made on the spectators that "never since the Execution of her in that yellow Ruff and Cuffs there hanged with her, was ever any seen to wear the like."[5] Her ghost, in cautioning vain women against wearing the yellow ruff, speaks of it, as Hawthorne does of Hester's letter, as an infamous badge:

> *O that my words might not be counted vain,*
> *But that my counsel might find entertain*
> *With those, whose souls are tainted with the itch*
> *Of this disease, whom pride doth so bewitch,*
> *That they do think it comely, not amiss:*
> *Then would they cast it off, and say, it is*
> *The bawd to pride, the badge to vanity,*
> *Whose very sight doth murther modesty.*[6]

Thus, each of these adulteresses stands out during her punishment on the scaffold conspicuously clad in a distinctive and colorful article of dress, created or invented by the guilty wearer. Each wears her scarlet letter or her yellow ruff for the rest of her natural life. And in each case the attractive ornament is called a shameful badge.

Hester's letter is equivalent to a fiery brand upon her soul. The people compare its color to the flames of hell. Because of its scarlet brilliance, the letter gives origin to a legend. In the vulgar mind, it "seemed to derive its scarlet hue from the flames of the infernal pit" (p. 91). The legend expands until the people believe that "the symbol was not mere scarlet cloth, tinged in an earthly dye-pot, but was red-hot with infernal fire" (p. 112). A similar comparison is made between hell's flames and Anne's starched yellow ruff. Niccols puts into the ghost's mouth an exhortation against wearing this garb:

> *Yea, then detesting it, they all would know,*
> *Some wicked wit did fetch it from below,*
> *That here they might express by this attire*
> *The colour of those wheels of Stygian fire.*[7]

Hawthorne uses the words *infernal* rather than *stygian* and *hue* rather than *colour;* he also stresses heat. But the concepts in both instances are identical.

Pride and vanity are distinguishing traits of Hester's character. The women at her punishment call her haughty and sneer at her bravery in dress. At her first appearance she recklessly repels the beadle (pp. 71-73). Hester's pride nourishes itself upon the skilful fashioning of luxuriant raiment. Hawthorne writes that "she had in her nature a rich, voluptuous, oriental characteristic,—a taste for the gorgeously beautiful" (p. 107). Somewhat analogously, Lady Frances is said to have been, besides lustful, also "prodigall of expence . . . and light of behaviour."[8] A closer parallel to Hester's pride and vanity is to be found in Niccols' depiction of the character of Anne Turner, whose ghost is made to say:

> *Two darling sins, too common and too foul,*
> *With their delights did then bewitch my soul;*
> *First pride array'd me in her loose attire,*
> *Fed my fond fancy fat with vain desires.*[9]

Hester thus agrees with Lady Frances and Anne Turner in possessing a voluptuous nature characterized by haughtiness and vanity. And like Anne especially, Hester appears to have exercised these attributes upon exquisite productions of her own inventiveness and upon vain attire for herself.

The scarlet letter is not only the token of Hester's violation of the social code and of her pride and vanity, but it also typifies her moral aberration in the spiritual world. In this badge Hawthorne depicts Hester's sin by means of witchcraft symbolism. The letter, as with a magic spell, encloses her in a sphere by herself (p. 74). She tells Pearl that the letter is the mark of the Black Man, whom she once met (p. 223), and twice she converses briefly with Mistress Hibbins, the witch (pp. 144, 286-288). On the first of these occasions, Mistress Hibbins announces that there will be a meeting of witches with the Black Man and urges Hester to attend.

This atmosphere of witchcraft enshrouding the character of Hester, in regard to her sin, agrees with the circumstances of witchcraft surrounding Lady Frances' adulterous liaison with Carr. To

51

Anne Turner, whom the narrator describes as a sorceress, an enchantress, and Lady Frances' second, went Lady Frances for assistance in obtaining the love of Robert Carr and inducing frigidity in Lord Essex.[10] In these matters of witchcraft and enchantment they turned to Forman.[11] When on trial, Weston confessed that Lady Frances had had dealings with witches and wizards.[12] Kempe mentions that she had had midnight interviews with "professors of the black art," and he includes in *The Loseley Manuscripts* an excerpt from a letter by Chamberlain which states that Lady Frances, "having sought out a certain wise woman, had much conference with her."[13] There emerges in this relationship of Lady Frances, the adulteress; Anne Turner, the witch; and Dr. Forman, the devil's agent, a design similar to the one in *The Scarlet Letter* of Hester, Mistress Hibbins, and the Black Man. Though without the intermediary figure of a witch, Niccols interprets Anne Turner, also a prototype of Hester, as having similarly had connections with the powers of darkness. He has her ghost say:

> *I left my God t'ask counsel of the devil,*
> *I knew there was no help from God in evil:*
> *As they that go on whoring unto hell,*
> *From thence to fetch some charm or magick spell;*
> *So over Thames, as o'er th' infernal lake,*
> *A wherry with its oars I oft did take,*
>
> . . . .
>
> *There Forman was, that fiend in human shape,*
> *That by his art did act the devil's ape.*[14]

Hawthorne's intimations that Hester has trafficked with the forces of evil thus have parallels in the conduct of both Lady Frances and Anne Turner. These two women explicitly dabbled in witchcraft to gain their lustful desires. Hester's connections with the Black Man are likewise related to her sin with Dimmesdale. Whereas Hawthorne, however, hints symbolically that Hester's sin was made possible through witchcraft, Lady Frances actually engaged in witchcraft to win Carr's love.

Hester's marriage to a physician (p. 94) agrees with Anne Turner's marital union with a doctor. Mistress Turner, at the time

of the Overbury crime, was a widow, but her former husband
had been a physician. She was, writes the narrator, a doctor's wife,
and during his lifetime George Turner had been the Countess'
physician.[15]

Hester is unhappy in her marriage to Roger Chillingworth. Her
husband lacks warm feelings. Not only is he old, but, it is implied,
at his age he is an incompetent marital companion. Hawthorne
compares their relationship to that of girl and old man, or that of
a "tuft of green moss on a crumbling wall" (p. 80). Reviewing
her early years of married life with Chillingworth, Hester holds
that period of her life among the ugliest of her remembrances.
Even when she married him, she had felt no love for him (p. 97).
In spite of the harsh circumstances of family poverty that prompted
her to it (p. 79), Hester marvels "how she could ever have been
wrought upon to marry" the man (p. 212). While he was absent,
not yet having joined her in New England, Hester thus yielded
to temptation and sinned with Dimmesdale. Hawthorne's portrayal
of Hester's unhappiness and faithlessness in her marriage relationship with a frigid husband agrees with the details of Lady
Frances' unhappy union with Lord Essex. When Lady Frances
was thirteen and Lord Essex was fourteen, they were matched
in a marriage to strengthen the ties between the Howard and
Devereux families. Immediately afterward they were separated,
Essex to travel, and she to remain at Court with her mother.[16]
Never having been thoroughly in love with him, as it seems, what
little affection she had for him died during his absence. She lav-
ished her love upon Robert Carr. Upon Essex's return from his
travels, he sought to live with his bride, who now found him
repulsive. With the assistance of Mistress Turner and Dr. Forman,
she used various methods of witchcraft to cause frigidity in him:
"pictures in wax are made, crosses and many strange uncouth things
(for what will the devill leave unattempted?) to accomplish their
ends, many attempts failed, and still the Earle stood it out; at
last they framed a picture in wax, and got a thorne from a tree
that boare leaves, and stuck upon the privity of the said picture,
by which means they accomplished their desire."[17] Having thus

53

succeeded, as she claimed, Lady Frances instigated divorce proceedings against Essex on the ground of his inability to "execute
the office of a husband." The commission appointed to decide
upon the petition ruled that Essex was unable to have copulation
with her, and they granted a divorce.[18]

The parallel with Hester's predicament is, by no means, an
exact duplication. Hester's husband is an old man, whereas Lady
Frances' husband was young. Lady Frances induced frigidity in
her husband, but Chillingworth has become debilitated by natural
processes of age. Yet, as Lady Frances' marriage was one of family
convenience with a bridegroom for whom she felt no love, so also
was Hester wrought upon to marry Chillingworth rather for eco-
nomic convenience than for love. As Lady Frances, moreover,
accused Essex of frigidity, Hester recalls with horror Chillingworth's cold heart and lack of warm feelings. And in each instance,
these unhappily married women engage in adultery during their
husbands' absence.

There seems to be a basic ambivalence in Hawthorne's portrayal
of Hester's repentance and salvation. With the characteristic uncertainty that inheres in life towards another's soul salvation,
Hawthorne, in contrast with his depiction of Dimmesdale and
Chillingworth, seems to fluctuate between condemning Hester and
showing her as having genuinely repented. He seems to doubt
her explanation for remaining in New England to work out her
salvation (p. 104). And concerning the notion of penance in
Hester's plying of her needle, Hawthorne remarks that "this morbid meddling of conscience with an immaterial matter betokened,
it is to be feared, no genuine and steadfast penitence" (pp. 107-
108). He again expresses a doubt when Hester harbors hatred in
her heart towards Chillingworth because of his vengeful conduct:
"What did it betoken?" he asks; "Had seven long years, under
the torture of the scarlet letter, inflicted so much of misery, and
wrought out no repentance?" (P. 213.) When Hester entertains
thoughts of suicide, Hawthorne states that the scarlet letter is not
performing its rightful function (p. 201).

Yet her life during her seven years of patient martyrdom elicits from the people much sympathetic respect. To many persons, the scarlet letter loses its original stigma. They interpret it to mean Able (p. 196). The "blameless purity of her life during all these years in which she had been set apart to infamy, was reckoned largely in her favor" (p. 194). Hawthorne himself observes on one occasion that Hester's struggle "to believe that no fellow-mortal was guilty like herself" is to be "accepted as a proof that all was not corrupt in this poor victim of her own frailty" (p. 112). In later life, moreover, Hester seems to outgrow self-commiseration and thoughts of suicide. She determines on a resolute moral course of action in order to redeem her error (p. 202). Even in her sins Hawthorne mitigates the guilt. He portrays her as badly matched with a coldhearted, incompetent, elderly man. In the forest, when she suggests elopement, Hawthorne lessons the crime by symbolically depicting in her hair a hope for happiness that seems basically rooted in the natural impulses of maidenhood. Hester's moral triumph makes it possible for her to say encouragingly to Dimmesdale that he has deeply repented and to speak of the value of penitence that is expressed in good works (p. 230). Finally, after Dimmesdale's death, Hester is said to have returned to New England to resume in the area of her crime, and in accordance with her earlier thoughts, a life of penitence (p. 310). Towards her and the other persons in her tragedy, Hawthorne remarks, following the example set by Christ towards the woman taken in adultery, that "we would fain be merciful" (p. 307).

The sympathetic respect which the people show towards Hester parallels the attitude of the people towards Anne Turner. In a similar fashion it was thought that Anne's repentance was genuine. She seemed to many persons to be deeply penitent. By her contrite exhortations to the spectators "to serve God, and abandon pride," she showed in her confession speech "great penitency," and "moved the spectators to great pity, and great grief for her."[19] Likewise, Niccols has her ghost ask of Overbury's ghost mercifully to "forget my great offence,/ Which I have purg'd with tears of penitence."[20] Anne's ghost, moreover, "with more compassion mov'd the poison'd knight" than did the ghosts of the other criminals, and after her ghost has disappeared, Overbury's ghost "did seem with tears/ To chide her fate."[21]

There appears also as conspicuous an ambiguity regarding Anne's salvation as is noticeable in the portrait of Hester. Anthony Weldon remarks that Anne died penitently and "shewed much modesty in her last act, which is to be hoped was accepted with God."[22] Amos reports that she herself had misgivings about her salvation: "She had, she said, been in the hands of the devil, (or to that effect,) but God had redeemed her from him, and that he had preserved her from many dangers in her life, wherein if she had perished, she had died more miserable for her soul's health than now she hoped she should."[23] Richard Niccols' interpretation agrees with these others. In a very crude distich, not likely to escape the notice of a reader entranced by these materials, Niccols writes that the ghost of Anne Turner "vanish'd from before our sight,/ I think to heaven, and think, I think aright."[24] Thus both Hester and Anne seem to have gained respect and sympathy by their penitential bearing. Both seem to have repented. And, though in both instances there is reservation and ambiguity, it is implied that the souls of these sinful women have been saved.

In summary, Hester's skill at needlework, her setting of fashions, her pride, the intimations of witchcraft enshrouding her sin of adultery, her marriage to a physician who is a "frigid" marital partner, and the merciful, yet ambiguous, treatment of her repentance appear to have parallels in the characters of Lady Frances and Anne Turner. Even Hester's scarlet badge, a product of her needlework, which she is condemned to wear on the scaffold and for the rest of her natural life, remotely coincides with Anne Turner's badge, her starched yellow ruff, which this woman was condemned to wear at her execution.

56

6

ARTHUR DIMMESDALE

PARALLELS between the story progression of *The Scarlet Letter* and incidents in the Overbury affair have emphasized the more significant aspects of Dimmesdale's role in the novel. Features of his character have been shown to compare with traits drawn from Carr, Overbury, and Helwyse. Both Dimmesdale and Carr commit a sexual sin. As a man deceived by a friend, Dimmesdale resembles Overbury. Dimmesdale and Overbury also analogously undergo the tortures of a languishing sickness. Dimmesdale's moral conflict and his guilty conscience for concealing a crime agree with the character of Jervase Helwyse. A few other similarities between Dimmesdale and these three counterparts also emerge in the literature of the Overbury case.

Dimmesdale possesses "high native gifts and scholar-like attainments" (p. 88). He is a "young and eminently distinguished divine" (p. 283), who has "achieved a brilliant popularity in his sacred office" (p. 172). Trained in "one of the great English universities," Dimmesdale brings "all the learning of the age into our wild forest-land" (p. 88). Even though young, he has gained a fame that is "still on its upward slope." It "already overshadowed the soberer reputations of his fellow-clergymen, eminent as several of them were" (p. 172). Dimmesdale's youthful eminence and rising fame coincide with the careers of both Carr and Overbury. Both of these young men were rapidly rising figures at the time of the Overbury tragedy. Their prospects as famous, influential politicians were great. Carr, in particular, had grown by royal

57

favor into a glory "so resplendent," writes the narrator, "that he drowned the dignity of the best of the Nobility, and the eminency of such as were much more excellent."[1] From a page in King James's household Carr rose to the rank of Viscount of Rochester. Many people perceived that Carr was destined for yet higher honors and that his reputation should eventually overshadow the prestige of others.[2] Later, in 1613, he became the Earl of Somerset, and until he was succeeded by George Villiers, he seems to have been the special favorite of the monarch.

Overbury's mounting fame at this time likewise presents a parallel to the youthful scholarly distinction of Dimmesdale. The narrator designates Overbury as a "scholar, and one that had an excellent tongue, and wit."[3] He attended Cambridge and studied law in the Middle Temple. At Court, he "found favour extraordinarily" and became "eminent and beloved both of the King and Councell," with "hope of better things" still.[4] Niccols has Overbury's ghost describe the recognition which Overbury had received and the success he showed promise of attaining:

> *I was (woe's me, that I was ever so)*
> *Belov'd in court, first step to all my woe:*
> *There did I gain the grace of prince and peers,*
> *Known old in judgment, though but young in years;*
> *And there, as in this kingdom's garden, where*
> *Both weeds and flowers did grow, my plant did bear*
> *The buds of hope, which, flow'ring in their prime*
> *And May of youth, did promise fruit in time.*[5]

Thus, Overbury and Carr are said to have achieved an eminence in their youth and, like Dimmesdale's, it was still on its upward slope. Overbury and Dimmesdale, moreover, have achieved comparable scholary prestige.

Dimmesdale's rise to fame is cut off before he reaches his peak because of a sin which, poisoning his system, causes his death. By his committing the sin of fornication, and by his concealing it in his breast, his prospects for an even more brilliant career are intercepted: "To the high mountain-peaks of faith and sanctity he would have climbed, had not the tendency been thwarted by the burden, whatever it might be, of crime or anguish, beneath which it was his doom to totter. It kept him down, on a level with the lowest" (p. 173). In similar fashion, the careers of Carr and Overbury were destroyed by a crime. Overbury, of course, was poisoned to death as a result of his interference in Carr's love affairs. Carr, on the other hand, because of his venery and more especially because of his share in the murder of Overbury, forfeited his glory. The writers of the documents relating to the case give their sympathy to Overbury. The narrator ruefully states that Overbury was "yet hindred in his expectation by some of his Enemies . . . all those good qualities obscured by the disgracefull reproaches of a dissolute woman."[6] The ghost of Overbury is made to say that "lust, foul lust, did, with a hand of blood,/ Supplant my plant, and crop me in the bud."[7] Despite the apparent differences between the situations of Dimmesdale and Overbury—and Dimmesdale and Carr—there is also a close parallel. Hawthorne stresses Dimmesdale's inability to attain the highest degree of religious exaltation, whereas the narrator emphasizes Overbury's ruined political prospects. Dimmesdale's own sexual sin causes his destruction, whereas not Overbury's lust but Carr's led to Overbury's downfall. But from a broader conceptual perspective, both Dimmesdale and Overbury are initially hindered, or thwarted, in reaching the summit of their careers, because of the crime of adultery. As a result of this crime, moreover, each suffers from a poisoning—one of conscience, the other of body—which eventually causes death.

There are indications that Dimmesdale has a scarlet letter A, corresponding to Hester's, etched on his bosom. The scarred flesh motif is fundamental in the portrayal of Dimmesdale's character. It emphasizes the essential guilty relationship between him and Hester. The marks symbolize hidden guilt, as Hester's letter sewed externally to her dress represents public disgrace. Engraved indelibly in the flesh, as Hawthorne intimates, Dimmesdale's bodily marks are also symptomatic of a fatal poisoning, which, originating from a spiritual canker, affects the body as well as the soul. By means of this symbolic—almost supernatural—treatment of the consequences of Dimmesdale's sin, Hawthorne motivates inter-action between Dimmesdale and the other major characters. Pearl, perceiving him constantly holding his hand over his breast where his pain is the most intense, senses that all is not right with him (p. 225). Upon pushing aside the garments of the sleeping minister on one occasion, Chillingworth, with diabolical glee, discovers a sight assuring him that Dimmesdale is his mortal enemy (p. 169). The marks, finally, are aids to Dimmesdale's confession of his guilt. Throwing back his vestments at his confession, he exposes a "ghastly miracle" (p. 302). Some bystanders testify to having seen a scarlet letter imprinted in the flesh; they disagree whether it was self-inflicted, whether it was caused by the "poisonous drugs" of Chillingworth's necromancy, or whether the "awful symbol was the effect of the ever-active tooth of remorse, gnawing from the inmost heart outwardly, and at last manifesting Heaven's dreadful judgment by the visible presence of the letter" (p. 305). A few onlookers, however, stubbornly claim that they saw nothing whatsoever to indicate a blemish on Dimmesdale's honor (p. 306).

The notion of mysterious, unsightly marks, shaped into the letter A, on Dimmesdale's breast and the people's opinions about them parallel the ugly blisters raised by poisons on Overbury's body and similar rumors concerning their cause. It was reported that during his incarceration Overbury "was changed in his complexion, his body consumed away, and full of yellow blisters, ugly to look upon . . . and upon his Belly twelve kernells, raised, not like to break . . . and from his shoulders downwards of a darke tawny colour, ugly to behold."[8] At his death were found more strange "botches and blisters on his body."[9] The narrator states that "thus venomously infected, appeared divers blanes and blisters, whereupon they to take away as well his good name, as his life, did slaunderously report, that he died of the French-pox."[10] Niccols' poetic version of this ghastly phenomenon likewise parallels Hawthorne's treatment of the scarred flesh of Dimmesdale. The ghost of Overbury is made to say that his foes foully defamed him after he died,

60

Arthur Dimmesdale

as they did kill
My body with foul death, that men might loath
My living name, and my dead body both.
False rumour, that mad monster, who still bears
More tongues about with her, than men have ears,
With scandal they did arm, and sent her out
Into the world, to spread those lyes about:
That those loath'd spots, marks of their pois'ning sin,
Which, dy'd with ugly marble, paint the skin
Of my dead body, were the marks most just
Of angry heaven's fierce wrath for my foul lust:
O barbarous cruelty! Oh! more than shame
Of shameless foes! with lust to blast my name,
When wonder 'twas, heaven's judgment did not seize
Their wanton bodies, with that great disease.

. . . .

Now, when false rumour's breath throughout the court,
And city both, had blown this false report,
Many, that oft before approv'd my name
With praise for virtue, blush'd, as if the shame
Of my supposed vice, thus given forth,
Did argue their weak judgment of my worth;
My friends look'd pale with anger, and my foes
Did laugh, to see too light belief cause those,
That lov'd me once, to loath that little dust
I left behind me, as a lump of lust.[11]

The differences in the two situations are great. Overbury actually had a hideously spotted body; it is only hinted and rumored that Dimmesdale has a letter imprinted in his flesh. Overbury's disfigured body was rumored to have been caused by venereal disease; there is no suggestion of this element in Dimmesdale's case. Yet there are also striking coincidences. Overbury's spots were caused by poisons; some of the people at Dimmesdale's confession contend that the marks on Dimmesdale had been produced by poisonous drugs administered by Chillingworth. Overbury's ghost laments that rumors had attributed to "heaven's fierce wrath" the discolored welts on his body as punishment for a sensual life. The ghost adds that "heaven's judgment" should have seized his foes for such slander. In similar terms, one rumor about the letter on Dimmesdale ascribes it to "Heaven's dreadful judgment." And finally, both situations are characterized by rumor and divergence of opinion in which some accept the common report and others do not.

Hawthorne's portrait of Dimmesdale implies that the Puritan minister is among the Elect of God and that his soul is predestined to salvation. Dimmesdale's predicament, in fact, seems largely to turn upon this aspect of his character. The artistic basis for his withering under a stricken conscience would seem to depend upon his having a saved soul and on his having a conscience. Thus Dimmesdale is depicted as a "heaven-ordained apostle" who possesses a deeply religious temperament (p. 147). He is a "true religionist" (p. 151) and a "godly pastor" (p. 71), on whom the people confer a spotless character. He suffers severely in his conscience, perhaps because of this innate sense of righteousness. To Hester he says: "Were I an atheist,—a man devoid of conscience,—a wretch with coarse and brutal instincts,—I might have found peace, long ere now. Nay, I never should have lost it" (p. 229). If he had been less righteous, if he had been an unsaved sinner without a conscience, Dimmesdale's remorse and acts of penance might have brought spiritual peace. But, confused and bewildered by his secret sin, he loses the assurance of divine grace. In his closest scourges, his introspective attempts to purify himself in order to see the workings of grace and to restore his assurance are of no avail. "With the superstition common to his brotherhood," says Chillingworth, "he fancied himself given over to a fiend, to be tortured with . . . despair of pardon" (p. 207). Yet, Hawthorne suggests that Providence was using Dimmesdale's avenger to bring about the minister's repentance—"and, perchance, pardoning where it seemed most to punish" (pp. 170-171).

Thus his conscience, in accord with the will of God, finally brings him to confess his guilt, and the clouds of despair vanish. Once again he has peace of soul. In this catastrophic scene at Dimmesdale's death-bed confession, his predestination to salvation seems dramatically to appear. Having despaired of salvation, having judged himself lost forever, and having tortured himself to purify himself, he is depicted in his dying moments receiving for eternity the full assurance of heavenly grace. His words pour out triumphantly his certainty of God's mercy and his salvation: "He hath proved his mercy, most of all, in my afflictions. By giving me this burning torture to bear upon my breast! By sending yonder dark and terrible old man, to keep the torture always at red-heat! By bringing me hither, to die this death of triumphant ignominy before the people! Had either of these agonies been wanting, I had been lost forever! Praised be his name! His will be done!" (P. 304.) [12]

Dimmesdale's receiving assurance of salvation in his last act has been shown to parallel Helwyse's similar experience. Helwyse's words in his final prayer also indicate a belief that his salvation has been predestined by God: "for were I not thine, then out of the root of me could not the buds of repentance appear, by wch I know thou lovest me; it is not I, but thou Lord hast drawne me to thee, for thine own mercies sake."[13] In a version of Helwyse's confession and prayer in *The Harleian Miscellany,* in the same volume with Richard Niccols' "Sir Thomas Overbury's Vision," this concept is stated more theologically: his comfort, says Helwyse, "is not any thing in man, no, it is *praescientia,* thy foreknowledge, O God, who hast elected me from eternity."[14] This version not only shows more clearly an agreement with Dimmesdale's election, but it also presents a parallel to the interpretation that Dimmesdale's sins had caused clouds of despair in his soul so that he could not see God's grace in himself. Helwyse prays: "Drive away this mist which is before me; and break those thick clouds which my sins have made, and may hinder my request to come into thy presence. Strengthen me in the midst of death, in the assurance of thy mercies."[15]

Richard Niccols' interpretation of the spiritual states of Helwyse and also of Overbury enables this comparison of election to be carried still further. The ghost of Helwyse is made to say that he had been "quit by death from doom of law, and heaven/ Out of free mercy" had forgiven him.[16] The ghost of Overbury similarly speaks of his having been saved: having called to God "For grace and mercy, after sad sighs given,/ With grievous groans, my soul fled hence to heaven."[17] And later this same ghost explains that he is not really dead, "for heaven such grace doth give,/ My soul in heaven, my name on earth doth live."[18] Thus, by emphasizing at their deaths their assurance of salvation, Helwyse and Dimmesdale coincide as characters. Each seems to have considered himself elected to salvation at one time, but, having lost his peace of soul by sinning and by concealing his sins from those who had a right to know, each comes to despair of pardon until his final confession. On this occasion each regains assurance of election.

In summary, Dimmesdale seems to possess several other character traits in common with persons in the Overbury affair. His youthful eminence agrees with that of Carr and Overbury. His scholarly recognition coincides with that of Overbury. As the careers of Carr and Overbury were intercepted by the sin of lust and the crime of murder, so Dimmesdale is thwarted in his rise to fame and to sanctity by his concealed sin and by revenge upon him. The suggestions of a scarlet letter imprinted in his flesh parallel the rumors of discolored blisters on the poisoned body of Overbury. And, finally, two of Dimmesdale's counterparts are depicted, like him, as predestined to salvation.

ROGER CHILLINGWORTH & PEARL

THE PORTRAIT of Chillingworth
that has begun to emerge shows similarities with each of the
husbands of Hester's counterparts. As a betrayed husband, Chillingworth has traits in common with Lord Essex, Lady Frances' first
husband;[1] as a revenging husband, with Carr; and as a physician,
with Anne Turner's deceased husband, Dr. Turner.[2] Chillingworth
has also been shown to possess a few characteristics of appearance
and profession in common with other men involved in the plot
on Overbury's life, namely, James Franklin and Richard Weston.
But these latter parallels need additional treatment.

Chillingworth is distinctively characterized by a physical deformity. On the scaffold, Hester pictures him in her mind "with
the left shoulder a trifle higher than the right" (p. 80). Later,
after renouncing her pledge of secrecy, she watches his "crooked
figure" depart through the forest (p. 213). Along with his deformity, Chillingworth is "small in stature" and has a dark
complexion (pp. 81-82). The shipmaster designates him a "black-
a-visaged, hump-shouldered old doctor" (p. 291). At least once,
these three features of Chillingworth's appearance are mentioned
together, in the phrase, "his low, dark, and misshapen figure"
(p. 167). Hawthorne dwells upon these traits with symbolic per-
sistence. Corresponding to Chillingworth's diabolism, they become
more pronounced the further the physician proceeds with his
sinister scheme of revenge. His complexion grows "duskier, and
his figure more misshapen" (p. 139). In these three distinctive

features of appearance, Chillingworth coincides precisely with the narrator's description of Franklin: "one Francklin a Yorkshire man was entertained into those actions, a man of a reasonable stature, crooked shouldred, of a swarthy complexion."[3]

A small man, Chillingworth also has a "pale, thin, scholar-like visage" (p. 79) which is deeply wrinkled by old age (pp. 81, 98). He wears a long, gray, grizzled beard (pp. 171, 211). There is a close agreement between these further traits of Chillingworth's appearance and Niccols' description of Weston:

> *A man of meagre looks, devoid of blood,*
> *Upon whose face death's pale complexion stood;*
>
> . . . .
>
> *. . . slender made, of visage sterne and grim;*
> *The hairs upon his head, and grisly beard,*
> *With age grown hoary, here and there appear'd;*
> *Time's iron hand, with many a wrinkled fret,*
> *The marks of age upon his front had set.*[4]

Besides coinciding with Franklin's appearance, Chillingworth's looks compare closely with those of Weston as well. The latter men are pale, thin, aging, grizzled-bearded, and wrinkled. While Hawthorne's words *pale, visage,* and *wrinkled* coincide with the diction of the poem, *thin* is synonymous with *slender,* and *grizzled* includes both *grisly* and *hoary.*

This wizened, disfigured old man is a scholarly doctor of physic. He describes himself as a "man of thought,—the book-worm of great libraries," who has given his "best years to feed the hungry dream of knowledge" (p. 96). During sojourns abroad, notably Amsterdam, the English-born Chillingworth had increased his store of knowledge (p. 83). His studies had made him acquainted with various branches of abstruse lore known to seventeenth-century scientists: alchemy, chirurgery, pharmacology, and necromancy. It is thus as a man of skill in "the medical and chirurgical profession" that he presents himself to the community (p. 146). His proficiency in antique physic includes a competent knowledge of the art of compounding medicines and drugs. He professes to know the various properties of simples (p. 94). He gathers wild blos-

soms, twigs, herbs, and roots for his concoctions (p. 202). He
converts weeds "into drugs of potency" (p. 160). He is believed
to be a conjurer and to have been seen in company with the
conjurer Forman (p. 155). He is thought to be a necromancer (p.
305) and to have engaged in the incantations of the Indian savages
and in other forms of the black art (p. 156).

Chillingworth's profession is comparable to that of Franklin.
The narrator calls Franklin a wizard and "a kind of Physitian."[5]
In another place this crooked-shouldered man, as well as Weston,
fulfills the description of an apothecary.[6] At the trial of Anne
Turner it is revealed that Franklin had learned from a "Chirurgeon" what was the strongest poison, with which he had allegedly
murdered his wife.[7] Richard Niccols has Franklin's ghost char-
acterize Franklin's studious pursuit of skill in physic and in other
natural sciences of his day:

> I was (woe's me, that still I was not so!)
> When April buds of youth themselves did shew
> Upon my chin, a student in the law;
> From which fantastick thoughts my mind did draw
> To the more pleasing study of that art
> Of physick; to the which though little part
> Of learning gave me help, yet strong desire
> To know that worthy science set on fire
> The fond affection of my forward will
> To search the secrets of that noble skill.[8]

Continuing, the ghost relates that in life he had gone abroad to
study: "the seas I pass'd to help out my weak skill/ In th' aro-
matick art."[9] Besides studying physic, the ghost states that abroad
he learned "with vain words to command/ The spirits from
below" and that, having returned to England,

> Forman, that cunning exorcist, and I
> Would many times our wicked wits apply
> Kind nature, in her working, to disarm
> Of proper strength; and, by our spells, would charm
> Both men and women.[10]

67

Thus Chillingworth and Franklin not only look alike, but they also think alike. They both possess a comparable scholarly frame of mind that eagerly pursues knowledge. They both spend much time abroad in studying physic and natural sciences. Each participates in incantations, and each is connected with the conjurer Forman.

Just as Dimmesdale appears to be predestined to salvation, so Chillingworth seems to be reprobated to Hell. At Chillingworth's first appearance in the novel, his depravity is symbolized by a snakelike distortion of his countenance: "A writhing horror twisted itself across his features, like a snake gliding swiftly over them, and making one little pause, with all its wreathed intervolutions in open sight" (p. 82). Chillingworth's scheme of revenge and his moral domination over Dimmesdale rest on an incapacity for forgiveness. Hatred in Chillingworth's soul brings to the fore his latent depravity of character. His major role in the spiritual drama becomes a diabolical one. Yet it is also providential; though he barters his soul "for a season, to burrow into the minister's intimacy, and plot against his soul," it is with Divine permission. By becoming Satan's emissary, as it were, or even Satan himself, Chillingworth torments Dimmesdale's conscience and brings about the minister's repentance (p. 156). But meanwhile, unhumanized by this malevolence, he himself degenerates into an evil fiend: "In a word, old Roger Chillingworth was a striking evidence of man's faculty of transforming himself into a devil, if he will only, for a reasonable space of time, undertake a devil's office" (p. 205). Having lived, therefore, by evil principles, Chillingworth at his death goes to Hell, for when "there was no more Devil's work on earth for him to do, it only remained for the unhumanized mortal to betake himself whither his Master would find him tasks enough, and pay him his wages duly" (p. 307).

Franklin presents a similar picture of a man with a depraved soul who has been damned to Hell. Richard Niccols describes the ghost of Franklin as among the condemned souls of after-life, "as a caitiff of that cursed crew,/ Whom sad despair doth after death pursue."[11] The ghost is made to say that he is possessed

68

with "that sly serpent of soul-slaying sin,/ Which feeds upon the guilty mind within/ Each wicked breast."[12] Concluding his speech, Franklin's ghost declares how he had been pursued in death by a fiend to be judged for his sins: "still the frantick fiend/ Did follow me unto my life's last breath;/ As was my life before, so was my death."[13] The narrator likewise depicts Franklin as a godless man. Once Franklin blasphemously retorted to a friend who had reproached him for his villainy: "Let them talke of God, that have to doe with him."[14] In comparison, however, Chillingworth is shown to have undergone a transformation. From a mild, but coldhearted individual, with a concern for human welfare (pp. 170, 208), he degenerates into a villain,[15] whereas Franklin's atheism and other manifestations of diabolism show his depravity immediately. Nevertheless, both men agree in being considered by their authors reprobated to eternal damnation. And, symbolical of their doom, at their first appearance each bears either within his mind or upon his features the image of a serpent.

Chillingworth, in conclusion, seems to be cast in the same mold with Franklin, physically, mentally, and spiritually. Both have crooked shoulders and dark complexions. Both possess a scholarly curiosity in natural sciences. Both are men of skill in physic and wizardry. And both men seem reprobated to perdition. Finally, Chillingworth and Weston agree in being small, pale, thin, wrinkled, and grizzled-bearded old men.

PEARL

Some facts about the life of Anne Carr have been shown to parallel the career of Pearl in the novel. They were both born in prison to erring mothers who were awaiting legal judgment for their crimes. The mother of Anne, a legitimate infant, had been indicted for murder and was awaiting prosecution; the mother of Pearl, an illegitimate child, was awaiting punishment for adultery. Anne Carr was taken from her mother before the trial, but Pearl's mother holds her in her arms during the three-hour sentence upon the scaffold. Anne was separated from her mother to be brought up in normal conditions, because Lady Frances, her mother, still had seven years to serve in prison. A movement gains force to deprive Hester of Pearl, on the theory that a fallen woman is not capable of managing her child's spiritual welfare; but Hester is, by the intercession of Dimmesdale, allowed to keep possession of her. According to the petitions made to the King by her father, Robert Carr, Anne became the heiress of her father's wealth; similarly, at the death of Chillingworth, her mother's husband, Pearl becomes his heiress. And when these girls reach the marriage age, they both marry into noble families and bear a child of their own. Very little about Anne Carr occurs in the narratives of the case. The records sketch only this meager outline of the little girl's life. It is, therefore, significant that for every detail of information about her in the documents there is a parallel in the factual history of Pearl's life.

It may not be amiss to note that Pearl's spiritual biography, her essential character, however, agrees with the attributes of Una, Hawthorne's own daughter, whom he described in his journals during 1848-1849. Nor should it be improper at this point briefly to include this evidence. Pearl is perverse, capricious, eccentric, and unamenable to rules, symbolical of her origin in a broken law (pp. 115-119, 215); her uncontrollable temperament compares with Una's eccentric and contrary disposition.[16] Pearl is a persistent teaser and tormenter of both Hester and Dimmesdale (pp. 122-123, 218, 253-254); Una, writes Hawthorne, is "certainly a most pertinacious teaser."[17] In this capacity, Pearl's role is angelic, that is, to bring to repentance her parents (p. 141); yet she is also like an imp, or an elf-child, and is said to have no earthly father but to be the offspring of demonic paternity (p. 124): "Hester could not help questioning . . . whether Pearl were a human child. She seemed rather an airy sprite" (p. 116). Likewise, Hawthorne characterizes Una as of supernatural in essence, both angelic and demonic: "there is something that almost frightens me about the child—I know not whether elfish or angelic, but, at all events, supernatural . . . I cannot believe her to be my own human child, but a spirit strangely mingled with good and evil."[18] Though Pearl possesses affections, they are neverthe-

70

less "acrid and disagreeable, as are the richest flavors of unripe fruit" (p. 216). Hester's hopes that her daughter will ripen into a noble woman are realized when at Dimmesdale's death Pearl sheds tears of sympathy that are indicative of a maturing woman (p. 303). Using a similar image to describe Una, Hawthorne writes: "she is as full oftentimes of acerbity as an unripe apple, that may be perfected to a mellow deliciousness hereafter."[19]

8

MISTRESS HIBBINS & THE BLACK MAN

IT HAS BEEN SUGGESTED that Mistress Hibbins parallels in character and in dramatic function the part played in the Overbury affair by Anne Turner in regard to the latter's assistance by means of witchcraft in Lady Frances' sin of adultery. To bring out Mistress Hibbins' role in the novel, these parallels need to be considered in more detail.

A widow and the sister of Governor Bellingham, Mistress Hibbins is also a witch (p. 181). Between herself and the Evil One, as well as between others and the Devil, she affirms a personal connection (p. 287). She is believed to be a "principal actor in all the works of necromancy that were continually going forward" in the settlement (p. 286). She makes excursions into the woods to attend witches' Sabbaths, as their meetings are usually called; she reputedly rides with other witches in Satan's company through the air (pp. 181-182). She speaks knowingly of Indian pow-wows and Lapland wizards (p. 287). For this infamous renown, says Hawthorne, she subsequently loses her life on the gallows (p. 144). From a few hints in the novel, it may also be inferred that Mistress Hibbins both was and still is Hester's second or mediator in securing through the Black Man's agency Hester's sinful desires with Dimmesdale. Mistress Hibbins, that is, may be considered as the arranger of Hester's first meeting with the Devil, upon which occasion, as Hester tells Pearl, she received in the scarlet letter the Devil's mark (p. 223). For, after the interview at Bellingham's hall, the witch explains to Hester that another meeting has been arranged between Hester and the Black Man (p. 144).

72

Mistress Hibbins & the Black Man

Anne Turner is virtually a prototype of Mistress Hibbins. A witch, a trafficker in necromancy, an accessible go-between for persons desiring contact with quacks and pretenders to occult knowledge, a sorceress and a whore herself, and an especial friend to Lady Frances, with whom she had been brought up, Anne Turner became Lady Frances' personal agent in the latter's attempts to induce love in Carr and frigidity in Essex. The narrator describes at length Anne Turner's wicked proclivities:

The Countesse of Essex having harboured in her heart envy towards her husband, even untill this time, makes her repaire unto one Mris. Turner (a Gentlewoman that from her youth had been given over to a loose kind of life) being of a low stature, faire visage, for outward behaviour comely, but in prodigality and excesse riotous, by which course of life she had consumed the greatest part of her husbands means, and her own, so that now wanting wherewith to fulfill her expectations, and extream pride, falls into evil courses, as to the prostitution of her body to common lust, to practise sorcery, and inchantment, and to many foul inconveniences, little lesse than a flat Bawd, by which meanes shee is made apt to enter into any evill action, to entertain any notion, be it never so facinorous. A doctors wife who was (during her husbands life) her Physitian. . . . The Countesse, I say, . . . repairs to her house.[1]

Anne, in turn, "being still her second," made Lady Frances acquainted with Dr. Forman, whose incantations, enchanted nutmegs, waxen figures, silver crosses, and other forms of his magic art gained for her the illicit love of Robert Carr.[2] At Weston's trial, his confession placed Anne Turner in a category with witches, sorceresses, and conjurers.[3] During her own trial were exhibited lewd pictures, puppets, crosses, and many uncouth items, the paraphernalia of her and Forman's witchcraft.[4] At this time, she explained her close connections with Lady Frances and how she had thought to befriend her.[5] Lord Chief Justice Coke accused her of the seven deadly sins and pronounced her "A Whore, a Baud, a Sorcerer, a Witch, a Papist, a Felon, and Murtherer, the Daughter of the Devill: Foreman"; he urged her to repent and to pray that God would "cast out of her those seven Devills."[6] She was executed, writes another author, for magic and witchcraft, as much as for procuring poisons in the murder of Overbury.[7]

Mistress Hibbins had been, moreover, an intimate friend of Anne Turner and a student of hers in the art of making yellow starch for ruffs. Returning from his forest interview with Hester, Dimmesdale passes the witch, who "made a very grand appearance; having on a high head-dress, a rich gown of velvet, and a ruff done up with the famous yellow starch, of which Ann Turner, her especial friend, had taught her the secret, before this last good lady had been hanged for Sir Thomas Overbury's murder" (p. 264). The significance of the starched yellow ruff has already been mentioned in the parallels between Hester and Anne Turner. Its reappearance here in connection with Mistress Hibbins serves to bind closer together the fictional relationship between Hawthorne's witch and Mistress Anne Turner, after whose execution for witchcraft the yellow starched ruff became a virtual symbol of her crime.[8]

The line separating the persons of Mistress Hibbins and Mistress Turner is a shadowy one indeed. Each is a witch. Each is involved in many acts of necromancy. Each is executed for witchcraft. Each seems to have mediated between a young married woman and the powers of evil and to have assisted thereby in an adulterous liaison. Mistress Hibbins was allegedly a friend of Mistress Turner, from her she learned the secret of the yellow starch, and in the novel she wears a type of Mistress Turner's starched yellow ruff.

THE BLACK MAN

A kind of vague witchcraft association in *The Scarlet Letter*, consisting of a reputable, though erring, woman, Hester Prynne; a disreputable witch, Mistress Hibbins; and the Devil, called by the New England colonists the Black Man, has already been compared to a similar cabal in the Overbury case, consisting of Lady Frances, Anne Turner, and Simon Forman. The precise parallels between the Black Man and Forman remain yet to be pointed out. The Black Man's few attributes center in a spiritual contract

74

involving the human soul. A compact with him means the inevitable forfeiture of one's soul in exchange for the consummation of some passion. In a request that her mother tell her a story about him, Pearl discloses the essence of the Black Man's character: "How he haunts this forest, and carries a book with him,—a big, heavy book, with iron clasps; and how this ugly Black Man offers his book and an iron pen to everybody that meets him here among the trees; and they are to write their names with their own blood. And then he sets his mark on their bosoms! Didst thou ever meet the Black Man, mother?" Continuing, Pearl explains her having heard from an old dame "that a thousand and a thousand people had met him here, and had written in his book, and have his mark on them. And that ugly-tempered lady, old Mistress Hibbins, was one!" (P. 222.) Mistress Hibbins, as Pearl observes, has long been in active league with him, and by this connection has attained not only much gossipy knowledge about people but also has acquired the ability to ride wingless through the air (pp. 182, 287). Chillingworth avows that he has in effect made, or soon will make, a bond in order to gain revenge on the seducer of his wife (pp. 99-100). Hester shrinks from becoming an active party to this contract, but she bears on her bosom a sign of her having at an earlier date met the potentate of evil and of obtaining through his agency the object of her passion (p. 223). Mistress Hibbins accuses Dimmesdale of making a contract with the Black Man, and the minister himself, by desiring to elope with Hester, wonders if he has not signed away his own soul (pp. 263-265).

Before demonstrating the similarities between this portrait of Satan and the magician Forman, however, it will be appropriate to notice, first, its agreement with Cotton Mather's depiction of the Black Man and, second, several attestations of the agency of the Devil in the Overbury affair. These details about the Black Man in the novel are consistent with seventeenth-century New Englanders' beliefs. Frequently the Devil is referred to by Puritans as a small, ugly Black Man. In *The Wonders of the Invisible World*, Cotton Mather states that in a witchcraft compact with the Black Man the first ritual in the ceremony is to cut the finger and with the flowing blood to enter one's name in the Black Man's book. To conclude the covenant, the Devil then leaves his mark on the signer.[9] Yet, despite Hawthorne's extensive knowledge of witchcraft, manifest by recurring witchcraft allusions in his tales and especially by such tales as "Young Goodman Brown" and "The Devil in Manuscript," Hawthorne seems not to have incorporated these data in his works prior to *The Scarlet Letter,* or afterwards.[10]

In accounts of the Overbury case, the narrator and others were convinced of the instrumentality of the Devil in the whole affair, but especially in the adultery of Lady Frances. The narrator writes that these deeds of magic performed by Forman and Anne Turner were witchcraft "practices, which as they were devillish, so the Devill had a hand in them."[11] And so when "certaine pictures of a man and woman in copulation, made in lead, as also the mould of brasse, wherein they were cast, a black scarfe also full of white crosses, which Mris. Turner had in her custody," were shown in court, and "there was heard a cracke from the Scaffolds," those present at the trial were afraid, "as if the devill had been present, and grown angry to have his workmanship shewed, by such as were not his own scholars."[12] The certainty of the Devil's agency in Lady Frances' marital situation was also stoutly affirmed by King James himself. In a profound discourse at her divorce proceedings, the monarch uttered an ecclesiastical and legal maxim that swung the weight of opinion in favor of the divorce. By asserting not only the Devil's undeniable existence, but also by defining the scope of the Devil's power in cases of sex, King James ascribed to witchcraft Lord Essex's impotence:

for as sure as God is, there be Devills, and some Devills must have some power, and their power is in this world, neither are the Elect exempted from this power; Job was not, Paul was not, Christ said to all his Disciples, *Cribaverit vos Sathanas;* and if the Devill hath any power it is over the flesh, rather over the filthiest and most sinfull part thereof, whereunto originall sin is soldred; as God before and under the Law to shew *officialem,* of purging mans originall sin, ordained the *praeputium* of the foreskin, and to

76

exempt this of our profession from the power of Witchcraft, is a paradox never yet maintained by any learned or wise man.[13]

King James, therefore, gave royal verification to the instrumentality of the Devil in connection with the sexual aspect of the Overbury case, for the Devil's appropriate domain, among the Elect, is the sin of the flesh, or the sin of passion ineradicably rooted in human nature. Likewise, in *The Scarlet Letter*, the sin of Hester and Dimmesdale, a sin of passion (p. 240), is ascribed to the Devil. But Hawthorne also shows the full extent of the Devil's power in depicting Chillingworth's bond of revenge as a witchcraft contract.

At least twice, moreover, in the documents relating to the murder of Overbury, Forman is equated with the Devil. Chief Justice Coke is reported to have called Mistress Turner "the Daughter of the Devill: Foreman."[14] Niccols similarly interprets Forman as an anthropomorphic embodiment of a devil. The poet has the ghost of Anne Turner picture him residing across the Thames, which is characterized as the infernal lake:

> *There Forman was, that fiend in human shape,*
> *That by his art did act the devil's ape:*
> *Oft there the black inchanter, with sad looks,*
> *Sat turning over his blasphemous books,*
> *Making strange characters in blood-red lines:*
> *And, to effect his horrible designs,*
> *Oft would he invocate the fiends below.*[15]

Not only is Forman called a devil, he is here represented as a "black inchanter" writing blood-red letters in blasphemous books. Kempe describes a notorious book of Forman's. For purposes of professional immunity, this magician and astrologer, Forman, kept a record book of all those who patronized his occult arts: at the "Countess' trial a book of Dr. Forman's was produced, in which he made all his visitors write their names with their own hands, before he would proceed to exercise his art."[16] Sir Anthony Weldon, in an extract reproduced in the notes in the *State Trials*, relates with a humorous twist a more detailed account of Forman's bizarre occupation, including the infamous directory of his patrons:

In the next place comes the countess to her Trial, at whose Arraignment, as also at Mrs. Turner's before, were shewed many pictures, puppets, with some exorcism and magic spells, which made them appear more odious as being known to converse with witches and wizards, and amongst the tricks Forman's book was shewed; this Forman was a fellow dwelt in Lambeth, a very silly fellow, yet had wit enough to cheat ladies and other women by pretending skill in telling their fortunes. As whether they should bury their husbands, and what second husbands they should have, and whether they should enjoy their loves, or whether maids should get husbands, or enjoy their servants to themselves without corrivals; but before he would tell any thing they must write their names to his alphebetical book, with their own handwriting. By this trick he kept them in awe if they should complain of his abusing them; as in truth he did nothing else; besides it was believed some meetings were at his house, and that the art of bawd was more beneficial to him than that of a conjuror, and that he was a better artist in the one than in the other, and that you may know his skill, he was himself a cuckold; having a very pretty wench to his wife, which would say, she did it to try his skill, but it fared with him as with astrologers, that cannot foresee their own destiny. I well remember there was much mirth made in the court upon the shewing this book, for it was reported the first leaf my lord Coke lighted on, he found his own wife's name.[17]

In other accounts Forman's books of magic are described. They consisted of disconnected pages, weird scrolls, and enchanted parchments. Among the possessions seized in his study at his death was a "little piece of the skin of a man." It was fastened upon one of his parchments containing cabalistic characters side by side with the names of the Holy Trinity. In another of his parchments was a "roll of Devils' names," devils who had been "conjured to torment the Lord Somerset, and Sir Arthur Manwaring, if their loves should not continue, the one to the Countesse, the other to Mris. Turner." It was these explosive scrolls of Forman's black art which, the narrator writes with the effect of identifying Forman with the Devil, that caused the scaffolds to fall at the trial as if they had been suddenly capsized by the Devil who had "grown angry to have his workmanship shewed."[18]

Thus, the Devil's agency in a sin of the flesh and a plot of revenge is a religious fact in both the novel and the Overbury scandal. Readers of *The Scarlet Letter* may, of course, regard this supernatural design as fantastic and superstitious; but historically the instrumentality of the Devil, as in the affair of Overbury and in the philosophy of the New England Puritans, was a truth of the universe. Not only do the tenuous suggestions in the novel of a witchcraft intrigue parallel an actual intrigue in the Overbury case, but in many ways the Black Man and Forman coincide. Each constitutes in the dynamics of the story in which he takes part a center of gravity for evil actions and also a point from which evil centrifugally flows. Though Forman is human and the Black Man is supernatural, each is conceived as an anthropomorphic representation of the Evil One, and to each in this capacity passionate sinners come for assistance. Each, moreover, has a notorious book in which his patrons must write their own names.[19]

Part Four

SETTING

୧ৣ৶ৼ 9 ৼ৶ৣ৸

TIME, PLACE, & ATMOSPHERE

A FEW ITEMS of setting in the novel have already been seen to coincide with similar details in the Overbury narrations. The market-place at Boston parallels the forum in Richard Niccols' "Sir Thomas Overbury's Vision." The kind of balcony or open gallery appended to one end of the meeting house for the magistrates agrees with the narrator's picture of the little gallery placed at one end of Westminster Hall for the Lord High Steward and his attendants. Some circumstances of time and atmosphere have also been stated or implied, but these and other data relating to time, place, and atmosphere need more extended analysis.

Hawthorne dates the story of *The Scarlet Letter* roughly in the 1640's with reference to at least five events, of which one is the Overbury murder. The action begins some fifteen or twenty years after the settling of Boston (p. 67), an event of 1630, that is, about 1645-1650; not less than two centuries before the writing of the novel in 1849 (p. 69), that is, sometime just before 1649; within less than half a century after Queen Elizabeth's reign (p. 70), 1558-1603, that is, sometime before 1653. Chillingworth's arrival occurs some thirty years after the Overbury affair (p. 155), 1613-1615, that is, about 1643-1645. Seven years later Dimmesdale stands at night on the scaffold, and on this same night Governor Winthrop dies (p. 192), an event of 1649. Though Hester lives on for many more years, the main action of the novel appears to be placed during a seven-year period that extends from approximately 1642 to

80

Time, Place, & Atmosphere

1649.[1] The month of June, in which, with Hester's punishment, the story begins, is definitely stated (p. 68) and is connected in a seasonal relationship, at least, with Lady Frances' trial on May 23, 1615.

With a chapter entitled "The Prison Door," Hawthorne opens *The Scarlet Letter*. Presenting a gloomy picture of the wooden jail in Boston's Prison Lane, Hawthorne draws special attention in three references to "the ponderous iron-work of its oaken door," to its door "studded with iron spikes," and to its "iron-clamped oaken door" (pp. 67-69). Gathered around this darksome edifice, with their eyes fastened intently upon the door, the people of the community await with a grim sense of fatality the emergence of a prisoner, Hester Prynne, who that day will undergo punishment for a crime. Hawthorne's description of the jail, with emphasis upon the iron-work of its door, seems to have an imaginative parallel in Niccols' description of the prisoners' dock at the Tower of London, in which the poet similarly focuses upon an iron gate. Niccols has just finished writing that the ghost of Overbury has appeared in a dream, has led him to the Tower, and has related his mode of death. At this point, writes the poet, as "Under the Tower's gate with me he stood,/ This accident befel on Thames' great flood." Niccols then describes the setting for this incident:

South by this house, where on the wharf fast by
Those thundering cannons ever ready lie,
A dock there is, which, like a darksome cave,
Arch'd over head, lets in Thames' flowing wave;
Under whose arch, oft have condemned men,
As through the Stygian lake, transported been
Into this fatal house, which evermore
For treason hoards up torturing racks in store:
At landing of this place, an iron gate
Locks up the passage, and, still keeping strait
The guilty prisoners, opens at no time,
But when false treason, or some horrid crime,
Knocks at the same; from whence, by law's just doom,
Condemned men but seldom back do come:

81

Part Four — Setting

(Whate'er thou art may chance to pass that way,
And view that place, unto thyself thus say:
God keep me faithful to my prince and state,
That I may never pass this iron gate).[2]

Niccols next proceeds to describe what happens. From the dock before him and the ghost of Overbury, there arise successively the dreadful shapes of four other ghosts: Weston's, Anne Turner's, Jervase Helwyse's, and Franklin's.

The differences between the scenes are greater than the similarities. Far removed from the little Boston jail in Prison Lane is this description of a part of the vast Tower of London, the arched prisoner's dock, through which flows the River Thames. The entrance to its watery passageway is barred by an iron gate, whereas the entrance to the jail in the novel is wooden. Nor do many of the subsidiary items in each description seem to have exact corresponding details. Niccols mentions cannons and racks of torture. Twice he cites treason. He concludes on a note of allegiance to King and country. Hawthorne, in contrast, mentions a cemetery. By adding symbolic weeds and a rose bush, he sounds notes of natural sympathy to condemned criminals. And he also introduces philosophical overtones of the Utopian ideals of the founders of a new country. Nevertheless, a few striking similarities exist. In each instance the place described is a jail. Each author draws attention to the door or gate of this jail, and especially to the iron-work of these inauspicious portals. Pervading each scene there is a comparable spirit of grimness and a sense of the awfulness of crime. This atmosphere of doom is conveyed by Niccols in such words as *darksome, fatal, condemned, horrid, guilty,* and *doom,* and by Hawthorne in *darker, gloomy, inauspicious, condemned, doom, grim,* and *awful.* Each description, moreover, is an introduction to the emergence of a criminal from within the depths of a prison. In the novel the figure of Hester emerges, and in the poem the shapes of four ghosts rise from the dock.

About three years after Hester's release from prison, she goes to the dwelling of Governor Bellingham. Hawthorne explains that Bellingham "had planned his new habitation after the residences

82

of gentlemen of fair estate in his native land," and that the whole appearance and taste were "of the Elizabethan age, or perhaps earlier" (p. 130). The walls of Bellingham's mansion, writes Hawthorne, have a very cheery aspect. They are "overspread with a kind of stucco, in which fragments of broken glass were plentifully intermixed; so that, when the sunshine fell aslant-wise over the front of the edifice, it glittered and sparkled" (p. 128). The walls are "further decorated with strange and seemingly cabalistic figures and diagrams" (p. 129). Entering, Hester and Pearl stand in a "wide and reasonably lofty hall, extending through the whole depth of the house." At one end of the hall is "one of those embowed hall-windows which we read of in old books." On its cushion lies a folio tome. On the wall hangs a "row of portraits, representing the forefathers of the Bellingham lineage, some with armor on their breasts, and others with stately ruffs and robes of peace." Near the middle of the hall, which is lined with oaken panels, is suspended "a suit of mail, not, like the pictures, an ancestral relic, but of the most modern date" (pp. 130-131).

These features of Bellingham's hall parallel some of the items in Kempe's description of Loseley Hall, where he found, among other papers, several documents relating to the Overbury affair. Loseley Hall, built prior to the Elizabethan age and remodeled about the beginning of her reign, is a venerable mansion of stone, writes Kempe. It, too, has a cheery, radiant atmosphere. It has a "lofty hall round which the portraits of its former owners are arranged, depicted 'in their habits as they lived'; the sunbeams stream through the light shafts of the lofty embayed window, illumining the household coats of the family, emblazoned in the gorgeous tinctures of heraldry on the glass."[3] Painted on the wainscot of one of its rooms is a monogram of the initials H.K.P., as well as a design of the heraldic device, the fleur-de-lis. The ceiling of the drawing room, observes Kempe, "is elegantly adorned with Gothic tracery and pendant corbels; a cockatrice is frequently introduced in the ornaments."[4] Lying in the chests of the muniment room are numerous folio volumes. The main hall is lined with ponderous oaken coffers. And "in the oriel or bay window of the great hall are the arms of More—Azure, a cross Argent, charged with five martlets Sable, with the date 1568."[5]

Not only do Bellingham's hall and Loseley Hall coincide as magnificent mansions, but the hall of the Puritan governor is said to be modeled on halls of the age to which Loseley Hall belongs, Elizabethan or earlier. And they agree on many salient characteristics. Each mansion is constructed of stone or stucco. Each is old or venerable. In each description there appears a cheery, sparkling light made by the sunbeams passing through or reflected by glass. Each hall is distinguished by a large "embayed" or "embowed" window—which, adds Hawthorne in explanation, "we read of in old books." Each structure is characterized by quaint, cabalistic figures, monograms, and designs. Each is lined with oaken panels. Folio volumes appear in each description. Around the walls of each hall is a row of ancestral portraits bedecked in their customary dress. Likewise, hanging in the hall is some species of armorial display, in both senses of the term. Where Kempe, however, stresses heraldry, the family arms, Hawthorne describes a coat of armor, the panoply of war.

The setting of *The Scarlet Letter* is distinctly characterized by a pervasive supernatural atmosphere, as well as by a natural locus of finite time and worldly place. The action of the story seems to be placed partly in the invisible world of spirit. Universal localities—Hell and Heaven—and spiritual essences—Satan, evil spirits, God, and angels—are an integral part of the setting. Yet neither the physical nor the spiritual world exists wholly apart from the other. Together they create an atmospheric setting. Their boundaries meet and overlap to form a unique twilight zone of the supernatural in which the two worlds have tangible connection.[6] In the forest interview, Hawthorne appears to symbolize the meeting of the two worlds in the mysterious brook. Dimmesdale fancies "that this brook is the boundary between two worlds" (p. 250). He compares himself and Hester to beings in the natural world and Pearl to an elfish spirit inhabiting the spiritual world. Elsewhere this spiritual world is presented realistically. Hell seems

84

to be as substantial a place as the meeting house and the market-place. Hester's scarlet letter, though a piece of cloth, is said to acquire its color from the glow of the infernal fire (p. 91). The darkness of Chillingworth's complexion is attributed to the soot and smoke from the flames of hell which flow into his laboratory from the lower regions (p. 156).

Satan and evil spirits seem to exist as living entities like the human beings with whom they intermingle. The Black Man lives in the forest attended by evil fiends, meets people whom he encourages to write their names in his black book, and presides over the Sabbaths of the witches (p. 222). Mistress Hibbins is intimately connected with the Evil One. She participates in devil worship with other of his converts (p. 287) and rides through the air in company with them and Satan (p. 181). Both Hester and Dimmesdale have had tangible intercourse with the Black Man, it seems, and bear on their bosoms the physical marks of their meeting. Chillingworth has the power of invoking devils and putting them to evil use (p. 156). The physician is also said to be Satan himself, torturing Dimmesdale, or Satan's emissary. At any rate, he becomes a fiend for undertaking a devil's office (pp. 156, 205). And Pearl's father is allegedly Satan (p. 288).

God, the upper regions, and the good spirits who dwell there are also realistically presented. God reveals himself to man through meteoric and other natural phenomena (p. 188). The hand of God, or Fate, seems to have interfered in Hester's removal of the scarlet letter and with the lovers' plans to elope (pp. 253, 285). Dimmesdale attributes the arrangement of his public confession to the will of God, and Hester and Dimmesdale long for life in Heaven, which they and the populace firmly believe to exist (pp. 303-304). Winthrop becomes an angel at his death, according to the devout Bostonians, and goes from earth to heaven to receive his reward (p. 192). Even in life the venerable magistrates are believed to have explicit fellowship with angels (p. 111). And Pearl's mission in life is compared to those angels of God who are sent to perform divine commands and to effect divine purposes (pp. 128, 303).

Part Four — Setting

Despite Hawthorne's predilection for suffusing tales with a supernatural atmosphere, as in "The Hollow of the Three Hills" and "Young Goodman Brown," the Overbury narratives provide a parallel to this atmospheric setting in *The Scarlet Letter*. Kempe gives a clear expression to the spiritual context in which the Overbury affair was enacted. In explaining the part of witchcraft in the case he writes:

A belief in the arts of necromancy is well known to have characterized the age; a creed which had the King himself for its patron, and rooted superstition for its source. Nay, there is little doubt that many practiced and studied it from a confidence in its efficacy, and thus really had dealings with the Prince of Darkness, as far as the gross impiety and turpitude of such attempts could place them in connexion with him.[7]

Concerning the death of Forman, Kempe adds that "the conjuror Forman was summoned by sudden death to that invisible world with which he pretended to have intercourse."[8] Richard Niccols, in his "Sir Thomas Overbury's Vision," also tacitly affirms the reality of this world of spirit and the fact of tangible intercourse between spirits and human beings. Though the poem takes the shape of a dream, the natural and the supernatural worlds mingle. A ghost returns from the other world and speaks to the poet. Other ghosts also enter his vision. Franklin's ghost is made to say that fiends have followed him both in his life and now in his death.[9] The color of Anne Turner's ruff proclaims the reality of Hell and of infernal fire.[10] Overbury and Helwyse alike have certainly gone on to Heaven, according to Niccols.[11] Likewise, in the narrator's account of the witchcraft intrigue and of the trial proceedings there is no clear line dividing the natural and the supernatural worlds. Forman had confederacy with the powers of evil.[12] The Devil actively participated in the case through Forman and, believed to be present at the trials, he caused the scaffolds to crack because his secret articles were being shown without due authority.[13] King James, moreover, testified to the Devil's instrumentality in the affair.[14]

86

Time, Place, & Atmosphere

Thus, several prominent aspects of setting in the novel agree with similar prominent features in the Overbury materials. The story is dated with reference to the Overbury case. Hester's punishment occurs in the same season of the year that Lady Frances was tried. The jail, the market-place, and the meeting-house in Boston parallel the Tower, the forum at Guildhall, and Westminster Hall in London. Governor Bellingham's mansion compares closely with Loseley Hall. The supernatural atmosphere of the novel also coincides with an analogous mingling of the natural and spiritual worlds in the Overbury narrations.

ᴄ🙚ᴇ 10 🙚ᴇ

DICTION, IMAGERY, & ALLUSIONS

O**BLIQUE REFERENCES** to stylistic parallels between the novel and the several accounts of the Over-bury affair have indicated frequent similarities of language. It is probably not a mere coincidence that the same key words appear in the novel and in the sources in the basic events, in essential traits of character, and in details of setting. One further coincidence deserves special attention.

The word *ignominy* recurs in the novel with the consistency of a refrain. Appearing in both explanatory contexts and in the speeches of characters, *ignominy* occurs no less than twenty-two times. Along with its frequently repeated synonyms, *shame, infamy,* and *scandal,* it helps to reflect the public's attitude of reproach towards Hester and her crime. From Hester's own point of view, it expresses her humiliating experience of public disgrace, both on the scaffold and her lifelong shame of wearing the scarlet letter. Her life is said to be one of ignominy (pp. 234, 290), and her punishment an ignominious exposure (p. 145). The platform of the pillory on which she stands embodies "the very ideal of ignominy itself" (p. 76). The scarlet letter on her breast is re-peatedly referred to as ignominious (pp. 75, 84). By this token she is, as it were, banished from society. Hawthorne writes that this "ignominious brand" (p. 110) was constantly the object of public gaze; although the world "could not entirely cast her off," it "made her feel as if she" no longer "belonged to it"; "it had set a mark upon her, more intolerable to a woman's heart than

88

that which branded the brow of Cain" (p. 108). The word *ignominy* also points up the contrast between her and Chillingworth and Dimmesdale. While Hester undergoes moral elevation by an open ignominy (pp. 89, 240), the two men degenerate through concealment and secret revenge. Chillingworth refuses to the end to share his wife's ignominy (p. 145). And not until the end is Dimmesdale brought by God's mercy to take upon himself, through a "death of triumphant ignominy before the people," the public disgrace commensurate with his guilt and Hester's shame (p. 304).

Ignominy is not a new or strange word for Hawthorne to use. He had used it in "Endicott and the Red Cross," in "Edward Randolph's Portrait,"[1] and in other tales. Its use also accords with his characteristic Latinized vocabulary, as exemplified in the novel by *somnambulism* (p. 179), *colloquy* (p. 239), and *multitudinous* (p. 255). Because of Hawthorne's penchant for the learned word, it may be a significant coincidence that the narrator uses the word at least three times, that Bacon uses it once, and that Jervase Helwyse uses it twice.[2] The narrator writes that Overbury was "brought into ignominy and contempt" by the rumors concerning his death.[3] Regarding Carr's guilty conscience, the narrator observes that Northampton feared lest their crime would come to light, their names be made scandalous to the world, and they "be branded with an ignominious death."[4] Again, speaking about the plans of Lady Frances, Carr, Northampton, and Weston to murder Overbury, the narrator writes: "thus being cockered up in their own conceipts, they run headlong to their own destruction; never remembring that were there but two persons privy to the act of murther, as in Cain and Abell, it could not passe unpunished, but that Cain must be markt with a perpetuall brand of Ignominy, and how much lesse should this goe undiscovered, when there are so many privy to it: Thus wee see that one sin, provokes another, and that murther is as neer to lust, as flame to smoak."[5] In similar language Bacon addressed the peers at Carr's trial: "For Murther, my Lords, the first record of Justice which was in the world, was judgement upon a Murtherer, in the person of Adams first-born Cain, and though it was not punished by death, but banishment, and marks of ignominy, in respect of the Primogenitors, or the population of the world, yet there was a severe charge given, that it should not go unpunished."[6] And, finally, Helwyse is reported to have said to the people in his confession speech that his death was, "though ignominious," a sign of God's mercy.[7] And in his prayer he gave thanks to God for bringing him to an ignominious death upon the scaffold rather than causing him to die unrepentant and unconfessed.[8]

In three of these five times that *ignominy* appears in the Overbury materials, the word is used to state concepts similar to those phrased by Hawthorne: a mark or brand of ignominy with reference to Cain, the notion of banishment, and associations of murder and adultery. Likewise, Helwyse's characterization of his manner of death according to God's mercy parallels Dimmesdale's use of the word in a similar context at his dying confession speech.

Three images in the novel, besides several already noticed, recall certain aspects of the Overbury case or an image in its literature. One of these, an image of crime and criminals in general, seems to point up some parallels already made between Dimmesdale and Helwyse. Dimmesdale argues with Chillingworth that the sinner may be justified for concealing a crime, though confession, he says, will give the sinner much relief. "How can it be otherwise? Why should a wretched man, guilty, we will say, of murder, prefer to keep the dead corpse buried in his own heart, rather than fling it forth at once, and let the universe take care of it!" (Pp. 161-162.) In the forest scene, Dimmesdale rationalizes his decision to elope with Hester by saying that, since he is irrevocably doomed, he has reason to "snatch the solace allowed to the condemned culprit before his execution" (p. 241). Having made the decision, he enjoys a feeling of exhilaration like the effect "upon a prisoner just escaped from the dungeon of his own heart" (pp. 241-242). This general crime image not only refers to murder, but seems to compare Dimmesdale to someone who has concealed the crime of murder, to someone who has been condemned to be executed, and to someone who has been a prisoner. These details recall Helwyse, who, after con-

90

niving in the murder of Overbury and concealing his guilt, was imprisoned and condemned to die on the scaffold.

The second image employs the notion of the trials of criminals before the judgment bar. After Hester is released from prison, she has doubts that her continuing love for Dimmesdale may prevent her repentance. Yet with him "she deemed herself connected in a union, that, unrecognized on earth, would bring them together before the bar of final judgment, and make that their marriage-altar, for a joint futurity of endless retribution" (p. 103). To Chillingworth, Dimmesdale remarks that guilty hearts must hold their secrets until the day of final judgment when all secrets shall be revealed (p. 161). Only at the great judgment day and before the judgment-seat of eternity, Dimmesdale tells Pearl while on the scaffold at night, will the three of them stand together (p. 186). The image occurs again when Dimmesdale stands up on the scaffold to confess publicly his crime: the sun "gave a distinctness to his figure, as he stood out from all the earth, to put in his plea of guilty at the bar of Eternal Justice" (p. 301). In the reports of the trials of Overbury's murderers the defendants replied to the question, who should try them, that they would be tried either by God and country or by God and their peers.[9] The judgment bar of eternity, however, seems to have a more vital reality to the characters in the novel than the earthly one which tried Overbury's murderers.

A third image in the novel specifically echoes an image used in one of the documents on the Overbury case. On the day of Hester's judgment, Dimmesdale tries to elicit from her the name of the person with whom she sinned. He says: "Take heed how thou deniest to him—who, perchance, hath not the courage to grasp it for himself—the bitter, but wholesome, cup that is now presented to thy lips!" (P. 89.) The image of the bitter cup appears again in connection with Hester's last, or so she believes, shameful appearance with her badge of guilt. She seems to endure gladly this last public gaze, as if to convert the agony into a kind of triumph. For at this moment when she foresees escape, she has feelings of regret about gaining freedom from the pain that had

91

become part of her being. Hawthorne asks: "Might there not be an irresistible desire to quaff a last, long, breathless draught of the cup of wormwood and aloes, with which nearly all her years of womanhood had been perpetually flavored? The wine of life, henceforth to be presented to her lips, must be indeed rich, delicious, and exhilarating, in its chased and golden beaker; or else leave an inevitable and weary languor, after the lees of bitterness wherewith she had been drugged, as with a cordial of intensest potency" (p. 271). A comparable image of a bitter cup appears twice in Helwyse's confession speech. As he stands on the scaffold at his execution, he points to some spectators in the crowd and entreats them to "beseech God to strengthen me in Death, though ignominious to some, yet to mee, a bitter cup mingled to me with Gods mercy."[10] After having spoken and prayed, he says fervently: "Lord I desire at thy hands, this bitter cup of death, as the Patient receiveth a bitter poyson, not once demanding what is in the cup, but takes and drinks it off, be it never so bitter."[11]

Since the bitter cup of death and its opposite figure, the beaker of the wine of life, are not original metaphors, it may be significant that the bitter cup image appears twice in a conspicuous document with whose contents many other comparisons have been made. There are, however, obvious differences in the uses of the figures. Helwyse's images refer to an ignominious death; Hawthorne's refer to an ignominious life. Helwyse uses only the bitter cup, and that crudely, while Hawthorne conjoins with it the beaker of the wine of life, and that with superb mastery of expression.

Several allusions in the novel to names of historical persons have been observed. The importance of Hawthorne's mentioning of Overbury, Forman, Anne Turner, and an unidentified companion of Forman has begun to emerge. The story of Overbury's murder seems to provide a commentary on the plot motifs of *The Scarlet Letter,* on details of characterization, and on Hawthorne's art. Allusions to Bacon, Coke, Noye, and Finch have been mentioned as being the names of legal figures associated with the Overbury trials. Hawthorne refers to King James, the monarch at the time of the Overbury murder (pp. 134-135). It has been seen also that *Cain* appears in both the novel and the Overbury materials, and in each instance the name points up the notion of a mark of banishment. Arthur Manwaring's given name agrees with that of Arthur Dimmesdale. Other names of people found in both the novel and in reports of the Overbury case itself, or in contiguous literature dealing with the age, might also be pursued—*David, Digby, Hester, Prynne, Chillingworth, Pearl,* and *Dimmesdale.*[12]

In Dimmesdale's study hangs a tapestried picture that tells the scriptural story of David, Bathsheba, and Nathan (p. 154). The allusion might serve as a comparison between the two holy men of God, David and Dimmesdale. Each committed adultery and each concealed his crime. Hawthorne's reference to this classic story of adultery and murder in a high place parallels references to it in the Overbury trials. Chief Justice Coke, at the trial of Weston, compared the Overbury affair to the adultery of David and Bathsheba and to David's murder of Uriah.[13] Elsewhere throughout the Overbury materials the connection appears again.[14]

Another name Hawthorne mentions is Sir Kenelm Digby. Concerning the mystery of Chillingworth's arrival, Hawthorne writes: "He was heard tó speak of Sir Kenelm Digby, and other famous men,—whose scientific attainments were esteemed hardly less than supernatural,—as having been his correspondents or associates" (p. 148). In contrast to the implied analogy between David and Dimmesdale, the allusion to Digby explicitly compares the scientific reputations of Digby and Chillingworth. Sir Kenelm Digby (1603-1665) achieved distinction in his age for researches in mathematics, philosophy, astrology, and other natural—and supernatural—sciences. In 1663 he was elected to the Council of the Royal Society of London. Among the more famous of his accomplishments, Digby perfected "the sympathetic powder," an alleged miraculous cure for wounds. He says that he learned the secret of this powder in Italy from a votary of a religious sect just come from Persia and the Indies "to whom he had rendered some essential kindness."[15] Thus, besides the general interest and achievement of both Chillingworth and Digby in the field of science, their specific learning of a secret cure from an "Indian" also coincides. Chillingworth explains to Hester that an American Indian taught him the recipe of the medicinal drug he offers her (p. 95). Moreover, each scientist learned the secret formula as payment for a favor—Digby, because of some essential kindness he had rendered; Chillingworth, "in requital of some lessons of my own" (p. 95).

The question arises whether there may not be, as seems to be the case with the Overbury allusions, further literary parallels between the novel and accounts of Digby's life. In 1827 was published the *Private Memoirs of Sir Kenelm Digby*.[16] The *Memoirs*, patterned along the lines of classical allegory, is written in a florid style. Two purposes of the author in writing seem to have been to give vent to religious, philosophical, and astrological speculations and to vindicate his wife's name from rumors of illicit love. The work is introduced by a prefatory sketch of Digby's life by the editor.

There may be a parallel between a forest scene in Digby's autobiography and several prominent features of the forest scene in the novel. As Pearl and Hester walk through the forest, Pearl questions her mother about the superstition of the Black Man and his book (pp. 222-225). Shortly afterwards, coming through the trees, Dimmesdale unexpectedly meets Hester sitting on a moss-covered tree trunk, where she is waiting for him (pp. 227-228). The whole scene is characterized by a hallucinatory quality. Hawthorne speaks of the meeting as a magic circle of an hour (p. 243). Dimmesdale wonders if the woman he sees is not a specter or a shadow (pp. 227-228). He regards the happiness of escape outlined by Hester as a dream (p. 237). After leaving Hester, he turns, expecting to find that she, too, has been unreal, for the whole interview has impressed him as being of a dreamlike indistinctness and duplicity (p. 256). Hawthorne, moreover, presents Pearl in the scene as if she were a vision of a child's spirit, brightly apparelled in the sunshine (p. 244). And he mentions that a prophet or magician skilled at reading symbolical char-

Good

acters could have seen that Pearl is, at once, the material union and the spiritual idea in whom are met the immortal destinies of Hester and Dimmesdale (p. 248).

These details—discussion of supernatural phenomena, meeting of estranged lovers in the woods, and a visionary atmosphere— seem to parallel a forest scene in the *Memoirs*. On his way to Alexandria (Madrid), Theagenes (Digby) joins company with an Indian Brachman, a skilful magician who carries with him a magic book enclosed in a leaden cover. The two men engage in a discussion of their beliefs in astrological influences upon human lives and in the interpenetrability of the spiritual and material worlds.[17] Once during the course of their conversation, Theagenes is halted by beholding the sight of his love, Stelliana (Venetia Stanley), sitting upon the "trunk of a dead and rotten tree."[18] But when he tries to touch her, she vanishes. The Brachman, coming forward, explains that the form of the woman was only a vision produced by his reading an incantation from the magic characters in his book. He had taken this way to prove to Theagenes that there is a general spirit of the universe that unites intellectual and material substances.[19]

In each work, a discussion of supernatural lore, involving the agency of spiritual essences in human affairs, is a prelude to a visionary meeting. In the novel, Pearl and Hester speak of a concrete embodiment of this lore in the person of the Black Man and his book. In the *Memoirs*, the Brachman, who carries a magic book, participates in the philosophical discourse. Dimmesdale and Theagenes are both surprised at the sudden sight of their loves, who are shown seated on a tree trunk deep in the forest. Both scenes are characterized by a magic circle or dreamlike atmosphere. Dimmesdale doubts Hester's physical existence and expects her to blur indistinctly into the trees; Stelliana actually vanishes because she is a vision. In a similar fashion, Pearl is described as the vision of a spirit. Hawthorne's allusion to a magician skilled to read symbolic characters parallels the magician's act of reading strange characters in his book to produce the vision of Stelliana. And Hawthorne's depiction of Pearl as the union of material and spiritual substances conjoining the destinies of her parents is virtually an illustration of the subject of the discourse between Theagenes and the Brachman.

Though not strictly an allusion, Hawthorne assigns to his heroine the same surname as that of William Prynne (1600-1669). Could there be any connection? Twice Prynne was sentenced to the pillory to be branded. In 1632, for writing *Histriomastix*, in which he slandered the royalty, he was fined, whipped, condemned to the pillory, where, after his ears were cropped, he was made to stand with a paper on his person declaring how foul an offense he had committed.[20] His publisher, Michael Sparke, the editor of *The Narrative History*, was sentenced to a milder form of the same penalty. *The Harleian Miscellany*, as well as the *State Trials*, includes a vivid account of Prynne's second punishment on the pillory—this time for slandering episcopacy. On this occasion not only were his ears cropped, but he was branded on both cheeks with the first letters of the words *Seditious Libeller*. When the executioner came "to sear him and cut off his ears," Prynne taunted: "Come, sear me, sear me, I shall 'bear in my body the marks of the Lord Jesus'; which the bloody executioner performed with extraordinary cruelty, heating his iron twice to burn one cheek; and cut one of his ears so close, that he cut off a piece of his cheek."[21] After the ordeal, Prynne composed a distich on the letters *S.L.*, making them to stand for the insignia of Laud, *Stigmata Laudis*, who had commanded the branding. Prynne became something of a type of the pilloried and branded criminal, the characteristic punishment of the age. The historian Oldmixon considered him a model instance of this manner of cruel and disgraceful public torture.[22] One of the early editors of the *State Trials*, Sollom Emlyn, cited the cases of Prynne as notorious examples of miscarriage of justice in the tyrannical use of the scaffold.[23] Prynne, too, considered himself something of a type. He told the spectators at his second branding that in order to preserve human liberties he would gladly expose his "person to be a leading example, to bear this punishment."[24] By giving to Hester the surname *Prynne*, Hawthorne may have been drawing

96

a parallel between the species of punishment on the scaffold which both she and William Prynne endured. The scarlet letter on her bosom, moreover, parallels the *S. L.* branded on the cheeks of Prynne. And frequently Hawthorne employs the image of the branding iron in speaking of Hester's embroidered letter (pp. 50, 110, 197).

Hawthorne gives Hester a Christian name that he had used, with the spelling *Esther,* several times before in his tales.[25] Like *Prynne,* the name *Hester* appears in the vicinity of the Overbury literature[26] and seems to point up a feature of Hester's character. One aspect of the scriptural story of Esther is once explicitly compared with a feature of the Overbury affair. When Sir Walter Raleigh returned from Orinoco in 1618 and was sentenced to die, he drew an analogy between his conviction and the hanging of Haman, and between Carr's pardon and Mordecai's similar royal release. Raleigh said, " 'That his whole *History of the World* had not the precedent, of a king's prisoner to purchase freedom, and his bosom favourite to have the halter, but in Scripture, Mordecai and Haman'; meaning himself and the earl of Somerset. To which he was told, that the king replied, 'He might die in that deceit.' Which he did, for Somerset was saved."[27] Both the Overbury murder and the Esther story were also touchstones in a popular controversy over woman during the reign of King James. Because two women, Lady Frances and Anne Turner, were involved in the affair, its antifeminist implications were strong. Overbury's poem "The Wife," allegedly written to dissuade Carr from marrying Lady Frances,[28] explains woman's place from the Christian point of view—exclusively a helpmate to man. After Anne Turner's execution, King James tried to put a curb on feminine vanity, apparently a phase of woman's self-advancement, by, among other things, outlawing the fashion of the starched yellow ruff.[29] Into this arena of controversy Esther appeared in the writings of the seventeenth-century feminists, as a symbolic champion of woman and the ideal of the equality of the sexes. The story of Esther inspired hope in the feminine cause. Not only did this wise and beautiful queen intercede for the deliverance of her people, but by her judicious behavior she removed the stigma attached to woman's place in the marital relationship. In spite of King Ahasuerus' official decree for active male supremacy, Queen Esther achieved an unexampled equality with him, and the golden scepter was extended to her.

Thus it may be that the name *Hester* is related to Hester's concern with the problem of woman's status. Besides the seventeenth-century spelling, Hawthorne gives the name overtones unsounded before. Hester is dark and exotic. She possesses "in her nature a rich, voluptuous, Oriental characteristic" (p. 107). Reminiscent of Esther, the deliverer of her race and an equal with her husband, Hester Prynne exercises her mental faculties on plans for the liberation of her sex. She imagines herself for a time as a prophetess leading a reform of woman's position (pp. 199-200). But in despair she concludes that the whole system of social relations must first undergo a change and that the destined prophetess who will reveal the higher truth for establishing marital relations on a firmer ground of mutual happiness must be pure, lofty, and sinless (p. 311).

Hester's husband assumes in the novel a surname identical with that of another seventeenth-century English figure, William Chillingworth (1602-1644). A liberal and an exponent of man's natural reason, Chillingworth typifies the new spirit of rationalistic inquiry that was coming over the age. John Aubrey describes him as a born debater and as the "readiest and nimblest disputant of his time in the university, perhaps none has equalled him since."[30] Lord Clarendon calls him that "learned and eminent Mr. Chillingworth," who had a sizable reputation with learned men of his age.[31] In his masterpiece, *The Religion of Protestants a Safe Way to Salvation* (1637), Chillingworth disavows partiality to system or conviction. He searches for truth, he says, in accordance with the principles of mathematical certainty.[32] He resolves the question of faith to reason and to the understanding's assent.[33] Roger Chillingworth has much in common with William Chillingworth. Roger is a learned man, a rationalist, and a liberal. He shrewdly reduces the problem of his calamity from one of human passions to a question involving "no more than the air-drawn lines and figures of a geometrical problem" (p. 158). He suggests to Bellingham and Wilson, to solve the enigma of Pearl's father and his wife's seducer, the rationalistic approach of analyzing Pearl's "make and mould" (p. 143). Chillingworth's cold liberalism is contrasted with Dimmesdale's "iron framework" of theological reasoning and warm religious faith (p. 151). It may be that there is also a symbolic meaning in Roger Chillingworth's surname.

Pearl's name has Biblical overtones. Hester named her daughter Pearl because she had been bought at a great price (p. 113). The name seems to have first originated in Hawthorne's mind, however, in another connection. He wrote in his journals that the name *Pearl*, the "English of Margaret," would be "a pretty name for a girl in a story."[34] In Kempe's *Loseley Manuscripts* occur several passages that recall this name. Listed among Mrs. Turner's belongings is a square of needlework pearls.[35] In the inventory of Carr's possessions there are, among buttons, hatbands, diamonds, also some pearls and a mother-of-pearl cup and cover.[36] In a letter by John Chamberlain describing Lady Frances' relations with witches, he writes that she "sought out a certain wise woman . . . [who] after the nature of such creatures, drawing much money from her, at last cozened her of a jewel of great value."[37] The adjectival phrase "mother-of-pearl" has a tantalizing parallel in Pearl's childish response to Wilson's question who she is: "I am mother's child, and my name is Pearl!" (p. 136). And, however it was intended, Chamberlain's statement of the "jewel of great value" coincides with the symbolic and figurative connotations of Pearl's name. Not only is she a pearl of great price, but she is also the "gem" on her mother's bosom (p. 272). These repetitions of the word *pearl* in one context in the Overbury materials could have reawakened in Hawthorne's mind the idea for a girl by that name and the symbolic meaning associated with it.

Dimmesdale is not a unique name, but there seems to be no apparent connection between Dimmesdale's character and men by that name in history. Three Dimsdales appear in the *State*

99

Trials. They are doctors John Dimsdale, Sr., John Dimsdale, Jr., and Robert Dimsdale, whose report of examination of the corpse of Mrs. Sarah Stout was introduced into the trials of that woman's murderers in 1699.[38] Several Dimsdales are mentioned in *The Gentleman's Magazine,* a periodical Hawthorne read regularly. The most distinguished seems to have been Dr. Thomas Dimsdale, who was honored by the Empress of Russia in 1769.[39] A Reverend James Dimsdale, Vicar of Cratefield, County of Suffolk, is listed in the obituary notices for the year 1793.[40] But, except for the last one mentioned, a minister like Dimmesdale, only the names seem to bear any similarity to Hawthorne's character.

Besides actual New England personages—Wilson, Eliot, Winthrop—who may be considered as taking part in the action of the novel, Hawthorne thus mentions or uses a number of names of English and Biblical characters. Each name seems to have some relevance to the novel, just as allusions in a well-wrought poem are integral to the poetic structure. Overbury and Dimmesdale each died a lingering death brought on by a deceitful friend. David and Dimmesdale were each guilty of a sexual sin. Forman and Chillingworth were conjurers and would-be destroyers of the soul. Digby suggests Chillingworth's scientific learning. William Chillingworth suggests Roger Chillingworth's liberalism and rationalism. The stories of Esther and Hester both involve the question of feminism. Hester Prynne and William Prynne both underwent the typical disgrace of the age on the platform of the pillory and carried the marks of their punishment with them through life. Moreover, the names cited or used may be found within the historical context of the seventeenth century and in the vicinity of the literature dealing with Overbury's murder. In the special instances of the names *Overbury* and *Digby,* literary parallels as well as symbolic associations seem to emerge.

ᏆᏏ 11 ᏏᏔ

STRUCTURAL DEVICES

Hawthorne introduces *The Scarlet Letter* as if he were editing the work of another author. The purpose of "The Custom House," he states, is to explain how the manuscript of the novel came into his possession and to offer proofs of the authenticity of the narrative (p. 18). He thus relates the circumstances of his bringing to light, among other old papers and documents in a second-story room of the Salem Custom House, a roll of papers wrapped in a faded scarlet cloth that resembled the letter A and seemed to be "an ornamental article of dress" (p. 50).[1] He observes that the document had been penned by Jonathan Pue, one of his predecessors as Surveyor of the Port of Salem, who was something of a local antiquarian (p. 49).[2] The pages, he continues, contained "many particulars respecting the life and conversation of one Hester Prynne," who had flourished in the mid-seventeenth century. Though he has adapted the story for publication, Hawthorne vouches for the authenticity of the narrative outline: "the main facts of [the] story are authorized and authenticated by the document of Mr. Surveyor Pue." But Hawthorne has not slavishly restricted himself to Pue's narration: "I must not be understood as affirming, that, in the dressing up of the tale, . . . I have invariably confined myself within the limits of the old Surveyor's half a dozen sheets of foolscap. On the contrary, I have allowed myself, . . . nearly or altogether as much license as if the facts had been entirely of my own invention. What I contend for is the authenticity of the outline." Moreover, "the original papers, together with the scarlet letter itself,—a most curious relic,—are still in my possession, and shall be freely exhibited to whomsoever, induced by the great interest of the narrative, may desire a sight of them" (pp. 51-52). And all of Pue's documents "shall be at the command of any gentleman, inclined, and competent, to take the unprofitable labor off my hands" (p. 49).

As Hawthorne says, the editorial introduction is a literary convention long recognized as proper by authors for explaining the existence of an ensuing production (p. 18). Daniel Defoe's *Robinson Crusoe* and *Moll Flanders*, Sir Walter Scott's *Waverley Novels*, Thomas Carlyle's *Sartor Resartus*, and Washington Irving's *Knickerbocker's History of New York* were similarly ascribed to other authors. Hawthorne himself had used the editorial device in "Rappaccini's Daughter" (1844) and in "P's Correspondence" (1845). Yet the Overbury materials are also presented to the public in edited volumes of antiquarian papers—*The Harleian Miscellany, The Narrative History, The Loseley Manuscripts*, and the *State Trials*. Of these works, *The Narrative History* may be singled out. Edited by Michael Sparke, *The Narrative History* includes, it will be remembered, the historical tract, "The Five Years of King James," and a large portion of the trial reports, "Truth Brought to Light by Time." Sparke prefaces these documents on the Overbury affair[3] with an editorial introduction that bears comparison with Hawthorne's account in "The Custom House" of the origin of *The Scarlet Letter* and the nature of this story.

Sparke reveals that the documents in his volume had been with much care and industry collected from the studies, closets, and cabinets of great men of state. Prior to his bringing them to light, they had been preserved, along with many others of like nature, by "the worthy Preserver" and "carefull Gentlemen G. W." Continuing his editorial task, he gives a faint notion of the nature of the story: "This following Story is worthy of observaton, for here is to be seen Gods justice, with punishments upon wicked sinfull wretches (both in judgement and equity) observe that what was here begun with vanity and adultery, ends in shame, infamy, and misery." For never was there "in these times such Sentence and Execution performed, as the then Learned Lord Cook gave on that fomenter of Lust, Mistris Anne Turner, whose Sentence was to be hanged at Tiburn in her yellow Tiffiny Ruff and Cuffs, being she was the first Inventor and wearer of that horrid Garb." Sparke next certifies that he has not altered the truth of the narrative and that any one who questions the authenticity of the story may come and inspect the documents: the narrative "goes neither with Patch nor Powder, nor new-Fashion dress, as that Carefull, Worthy and Learned Licenser can shew, not detracted nor added one line to the matter, from the Original. And if any Gentleman or man of Quality shall make doubt, . . . we have done according to the Original Copy, and if they be desirous to see the Originals, . . . they shall have leave to see them."[4]

Thus, both *The Scarlet Letter* and the main Overbury narrative are said by their "editors" to be documents by another author. Each story is alleged to have been collected and preserved among numerous papers by a kind of antiquarian, Pue and G. W. Neither editor gives a very full preview of the ensuing narrative; each mentions only the name of one principal character and a detail about an infamous article of dress made and worn by her—Hester and the scarlet letter, Anne Turner and the starched yellow ruff. Sparke, in contrast to Hawthorne, does cite a theme word, *adultery*, and points out moral implications of the narrative. Each editor vouches for the authenticity of the story. But, while Sparke claims not to have given it a new dress by altering a single line, as the "licenser" can testify, Hawthorne claims that he has, though keeping to the factual outline, allowed himself considerable interpretative "license" in dressing up the tale. Each editor also points out, finally, that the original papers are at the disposal of any gentleman who desires a sight of them—because of interest in the novel or because of doubt as to the truth of the facts.

In the novel, Hawthorne retains the editorial point of view by at least two means. First, he reminds the reader by parenthetical references to it that he is following a prepared document. When one day Mistress Hibbins tells Hester of a witch meeting to be held that night, Hawthorne interpolates: "if we suppose this interview betwixt Mistress Hibbins and Hester Prynne to be authentic, and not a parable" (p. 144). Comparing Chillingworth to a companion of Forman, Hawthorne writes that the "narrator of the story had now forgotten" this companion's name (p. 155). Of a wolf's friendly conduct towards Pearl during the girl's amble in the forest, he observes: "but here the tale has surely lapsed into the improbable" (p. 245). And after Dimmesdale's death, Hawthorne mentions again "the authority which we have chiefly followed,—a manuscript of old date" (p. 307) and its supposed author, "Mr. Surveyor Pue, who made investigations a century later" (p. 310).

The second means of continuing the editorial perspective is to take full advantage of the opportunities afforded him to make comments of general interest arising from the story. These observations pertain to history, religion, philosophy, morals, religion, human nature, and other general areas. Regarding punishment on the pillory, for example, he remarks: "There can be no outrage, methinks, against our common nature, . . . no outrage more flagrant than to forbid the culprit to hide his face for shame" (p. 76). Many other passages may similarly be lifted out of context:

But there is a fatality, . . . which almost invariably compels human beings to linger around . . . the spot where some . . . marked event has given the color to their lifetime (p. 103).

. . . loss of faith is ever one of the saddest results of sin (p. 112).

So it ever is, whether thus typified or no, that an evil deed invests itself with the character of doom (p. 253).

Be true! Be true! Be true! Show freely to the world, if not your worst, yet some trait whereby the worst may be inferred! (P. 307.)

Hawthorne's editorial point of view in the novel parallels the perspective of the anonymous narrator of "The Five Years" more than that of Sparke, for the latter, in accord with his prefatory statement, remains out of the narrative. In only one place Sparke's presence is conspicuous. The narrator had said, concerning the trials of the accomplices, that "to write the particulars of their arraignments, confessions, and the manner of their deaths is needless, being common."[5] But Sparke, in a phrase that anticipates the second part of the volume, alters the passage to read: "the particulars of their Arraignments, Confessions, and the manner of their Deaths I have set downe by it selfe in the latter end of this Treatise, being both needfull and necessary for the clearing of the whole truth of this businesse, to take away those ambiguous doubts that did arise of the certainty thereof."[6]

But, despite the convention of generalizations, moral and philosophical, among English novelists of the eighteenth century, and despite Hawthorne's own custom in early tales,[7] this characteristic of Hawthorne's style also coincides with the practice of the narrator, who frequently injects moral maxims into his story:

. . . for who can touch pitch and not be defiled?[8]

Many are the chances that happen in the world, some good, some bad, and those things we least suspect doe soonest happen to subvert us.[9]

Hereby it is a dangerous thing to fall within the compasse of a guilty conscience, it eateth and consumeth the soule of a man, as rust the iron, or as beating waves the hollow rocks.[10]

But what God will have disclosed shall never be concealed.[11]

. . . God never leaves Murther (though never so closely carryed) Undiscovered, and Unpunished.[12]

And, in this last quotation, the narrator concludes, as Hawthorne does, with a pointed moral.

Hawthorne adapts his edited story within the imaginary framework of a visitation by Pue's ghost. As he examined Pue's manuscript, he had a feeling, he says, that there stood before him the ghost of its author, who handed him the document and requested him to redact it for publication:

It impressed me as if the ancient Surveyor . . . had met me in the deserted chamber of the Custom House. . . . With his own ghostly hand, the obscurely seen but majestic figure had imparted to me the scarlet symbol, and the little roll of explanatory manuscript. With his own ghostly voice he had exhorted me, on the sacred consideration of my filial duty and reverence towards him, . . . to bring his mouldy and moth-eaten lucubrations before the public. "Do this," said the ghost of Mr. Surveyor Pue, . . . "do this, and the profit shall be all your own! . . . But, I charge you, in this matter of old Mistress Prynne, give to your predecessor's memory the credit which will be rightfully due!" And I said to the ghost of Mr. Surveyor Pue, "I will!" (Pp. 52-53.)

Further, the characters of the story are compared to ghosts in the early stages of their creation. Hawthorne writes that his imagination would not function while working in the Custom House: "The characters of the narrative would not be warmed and rendered malleable by any heat that I could kindle at my intellectual forge. They would take neither the glow of passion nor the tenderness of sentiment, but retained all the rigidity of dead corpses, and stared me in the face with a fixed and ghastly grin of contemptuous defiance" (pp. 53-54). Not until he was discharged from the Custom House and was able in his study to dream strange dreams amidst the ruddy glow of coal-fire light and moonbeams, he says, were the ghosts spiritualized into human beings with hearts and sensibilities.

Even in the completed narrative the characters are often represented figuratively as ghosts or disembodied spirits. After her virtual banishment, Hester's features show a marble quietude: they are "like a mask; or, rather, like the frozen calmness of a dead woman's features; owing this dreary resemblance to the fact that Hester was actually dead, in respect to any claim of sympathy, and had departed out of the world, with which she still seemed to mingle" (p. 270). For Hester "stood apart from moral interests, yet close beside them, like a ghost that revisits the familiar fireside" (p. 108). As he sees Bellingham from a distance looking "like a ghost, evoked unseasonably from the grave" (p. 181), Dimmesdale imagines that he himself may be taken for the "ghost . . . of some defunct transgressor," if he be found frozen the next morning (p. 184). The meeting of Hester and Dimmesdale in the woods after seven years is "like the first encounter, in the world beyond the grave, of two spirits who had been intimately connected in their former life, but now stood coldly shuddering, in mutual dread; as not yet familiar with their state, nor wonted to the companionship of disembodied beings. Each a ghost, and awe-stricken at the other ghost!" (P. 228.) At the Election holiday, Dimmesdale's face has such a deathlike hue that it seems "hardly the face of a man alive" (p. 297); he regards Hester and Pearl with a ghastly look (p. 299). In this world of spirits, Chillingworth figures as an evil fiend (pp. 205, 207) and Pearl an elf-child (pp. 115, 136).

Hawthorne had employed the device of the dream framework in "Young Goodman Brown" (1835) and in "David Swan" (1837). He had used the joint ghost-dream structure in "An Old Woman's Tale" (1830) and in "Wives of the Dead" (1832). In "The Old Manse" he had anticipated the imaginary appearance of a ghost who desires him to edit a manuscript: Hawthorne speaks frequently in this sketch of the ghost of Dr. Ezra Ripley, whose house he had rented. Once fancying he hears the ghost rustling papers, he assumes: "Not improbably he wished me to edit and publish a selection from a chest full of manuscript discourses that stood in the garret."[13] Students of Romanticism are also well aware that ghost and spirit imagery is a trademark of the literature of that idealistic attitude toward life.

Nevertheless, there is a parallel between this imaginary ghost-vision framework of the novel and the structural framework of Richard Niccols' "Sir Thomas Overbury's Vision." Niccols has returned from the forum and has gone to bed. In his sleep he has a dream. There appears to him around midnight the ghost of Overbury:

> *Just at that hour,*[14] *I thought my chamber door*
> *Did softly open, and upon the floor*
> *I heard one glide along, who at the last*
> *Did call ad [sic] bid me wake; at which aghast*
> *I up did look.*

. . . .
But the poor ghost, to let me understand
For what he came, did waft me with his hand.[15]

Bidding him rise, the ghost leads him to Tower Hill and tells him
how in life he was poisoned to death and disgracefully slandered
by false rumors. It is to request of the poet that he tell the true
story of Overbury's misfortunes, and thus vindicate his character,
the ghost declares, that he has left his grave and stolen "through
covert shades of night, to crave/ Thy pen's assistance."[16] The
narration continues with the successive[17] appearance out of the
prisoners' dock of the ghosts of Overbury's murderers. After the
last one has disappeared and the ghost of Overbury has thanked
King James for justice in apprehending the murderers, writes
Niccols, he wakes up and concludes the poem with: "this vision
I did write."[18]

In contrast to Niccols' structure, in which a ghost is said actually
to have appeared to the poet in a dream, Hawthorne employs
the device figuratively; he imagines the spectral figure of Pue
standing before him, he merely compares the characters to ghosts,
and he hints at a dream only once and in general terms. Niccols
makes the ghost-dream framework an integral part of the narrative
structure of the poem, whereas Hawthorne places the ghost's
appearance and request before the main narration in connection
with the editorial framework. Yet in each work the author says
that he is bringing to the public a story at the request of a ghost
who has appeared to him. Each ghost is shown asking that the
treatment duly regard the memory of his name. And in each
instance there is a picture of a ghost standing in a chamber with
his hand extended, either to beckon the poet to follow or to
impart the manuscript to the novelist.

Pue, explains Hawthorne in "The Custom House," had drawn
up the narration of Hester Prynne from the oral testimony of
persons who had lived at the time of her disgrace (p. 51). Hawthorne retains this principle of rumor and gossip as the basis of
the narrative structure of the novel. The story moves forward
from the point of view of the populace, whose gossipy opinions

color the facts. This device of reporting rumor gives to the style
of the novel a popular flavor:

It was whispered . . . (p. 91).

The vulgar, who, in those dreary old times, were always con-
tributing a grotesque horror to what interested their imaginations,
had a story . . . which we might readily work up into a terrific
legend. . . . They averred. . . . And we must needs say . . . that
perhaps there was more truth in the rumor than our modern in-
credulity may be inclined to admit (p. 112).

According to the vulgar idea . . . (p. 156).

. . . it grew to be a widely diffused opinion . . . (p. 156).

It was reported, and believed by many . . . (p. 197).

. . . the market-place absolutely babbled, from side to side. . . .
According to their united testimony . . . (p. 294).

. . . no tidings . . . unquestionably authentic were received (p.
309).

In fine, the gossips of that day believed . . . (p. 310).

These illustrations of Hawthorne's device of reporting popular
opinions[19] compare with the gossipy style of the narrator. This
anonymous author writes as if oral testimony were his only sources
of information on the subjects he covers. Referring to almost no
authorities, he keeps completely on the level of the uninformed
but gossiping people. He repeats the news from spectators and
the hearsay evidence from nonspectators. He includes the rumors,
the opinions, and all the unverifiable reports of the multitude.
His style is distinctly characterized by rumor-mongering:

. . . it was vulgarly reported . . .[20]

. . . an idle and vain rumor that was spread . . .[21]

. . . and besides, which is now the common report of the vulgar . . .[22]

. . . as was reported . . .[23]

. . . although many had been the rumors and reports that had
passed in these times, some of them shoot up for uncertain truths,
and flying tales . . .[24]

And the tongues of the Vulgar began to walke . . .[25]

Frequently in the novel there are conflicting opinions among the rumors of the people. Hawthorne presents these different views in a stylistic formula that has been called multiple-choice explanations. By this device, says F. O. Matthiessen, Hawthorne conveys an atmosphere of mystery and obscurity, and creates "a sense of the intricacy" of the situations reported:[26]

By those best acquainted . . . [it] was accounted for by. . . . Some declared. . . . He himself . . . avowed his belief. . . . With all this difference of opinion as to the cause . . . there could be no question of the fact . . . (pp. 147-148).

His first entry on the scene, few people could tell whence, dropping down . . . out of the sky, or starting from the nether earth . . . a rumor gained ground,—and, however absurd, was entertained by some very sensible people. . . . Individuals of wiser faith, indeed . . . (pp. 148-149).

. . . friends . . . very reasonably imagined. . . . But—it must now be said—another portion of the community had latterly begun to take its own view. . . . The people, in the case of which we speak, could justify its prejudice . . . by no fact or argument worthy of serious refutation. There was an aged handicraftsman . . . [who] testified to. . . . Two or three individuals hinted. . . . A large number—and many of these were persons of such sober sense and practical observation that their opinions would have been valuable in other matters—affirmed . . . (pp. 155-156).

After many days, when time sufficed for the people to arrange their thoughts in reference to the foregoing scene, there was more than one account of what had been witnessed. . . . Most of the spectators testified to having seen. . . . As regarded its origin, there were various explanations, all of which must necessarily have been conjectural. Some affirmed. . . . Others contended. . . . Others, again, . . . whispered their belief. . . . The reader may choose among these theories. . . . It is singular, nevertheless, that certain persons, who were spectators of the whole scene . . . denied . . . (pp. 305-306).

In the same manner precisely, the narrator presents contradictory rumors of the people.[27] His basic stylistic pattern, in fact, may be said to consist of crudely multiplying the various popular opinions:

Strange was the accident, and many the rumors that issued. . . . Some said . . .; others, that he was . . .; again, others thought . . .; yet no certainty could be found. . . .[28]
. . . whereupon some saies this, and some saies that, and most that the . . . , but how true this is, is not credible. . . .[29]
. . . it was thought . . . he was thought . . . another was . . . but the very truth of the businesse was thought to be this.[30]
And now according to the common course, every one speaks as they stand affected, some boldly, some sparingly: some. . . . Others. . . . A third sort. . . . Others, that were more staid and judicious in their opinions, foresaw. . . .[31]
After [wards] it was given out, that. . . . This went for currant amongst some, amongst others that were ignorant some little respect they had to it, but to others that sought narrower into the matter, they found it far otherwise.[32]

Thus, in both *The Narrative History* and *The Scarlet Letter* there is a triple stratification of authorship. The outside layer is by an editor who, in adapting the narration of another author, writes an introduction and makes generalizing comments on various subjects as he retells the story. The second layer is the narration of a scribbler who has collected his materials from the oral testimony of many individuals. These opinions and rumors of the uninstructed multitude constitute the third layer of authorship, through whose eyes, for the most part, the story is told. The styles of both narrations are, therefore, gossipy and characterized by contradictory reports. Each narrator, in presenting a series of these rumors, frequently tries to evaluate the reliability of the opinions. Because of these conflicting views, each story possesses an atmosphere of mystery and uncertainty. Moreover, Hawthorne's editorial superstructure, which includes the visitation of a ghost and also involves ghostly characters, especially as the story begins to take shape, recalls the appearance of Overbury's ghost to Niccols and the ghost-dream framework of Niccols' poem.

111

᚛ᚌ 12 ᚕᚋᚐ

STATIC SYMBOL
TO NARRATIVE MEANING

I̤T HAS BEEN the purpose of the preceding chapters to suggest that accounts of the murder of Sir Thomas Overbury were Hawthorne's principal sources in composing *The Scarlet Letter*. The main points in the argument may be briefly recapitulated. In the novel, Hawthorne twice alludes to the Overbury murder. He mentions the names of several other persons implicated in the case or involved in the trials. In their broad outlines of adultery, witchcraft, isolation, revenge, violation of a human soul, concealed sin, dying confession, and divine judgment upon sinners, *The Scarlet Letter* and the Overbury affair share common motifs. Hawthorne was acquainted with the literature of the period, and especially with books carrying accounts of the affair. He knew *The Harleian Miscellany*, which contains a historical tract, "The Five Years of King James," and a poem by Richard Niccols, "Sir Thomas Overbury's Vision." The tract narrates anonymously the basic facts in the case; the poem is an imaginative and more penetrating character study of the accomplices who, as ghosts, are shown confessing their crime to the ghost of Overbury. Hawthorne knew the *State Trials*. He knew Michael Sparke's *The Narrative History*, which includes the tract and a large portion of the trial reports. He knew Alfred John Kempe's *The Loseley Manuscripts*, which contains a narration of the affair and several documents relating to it. And about the time he was writing the novel, records of Hawthorne's reading at the Salem Athenaeum have shown, he was using *The Loseley Manu-*

scripts and an edition of *The Harleian Miscellany*—one, however, that contains the tract but not the poem.

A detailed comparative analysis of the plotlines of the novel and these accounts of the case has revealed, though not in identical order, many incidents common to both stories. Striking agreements between the major characters in the novel and the Overbury affair have emerged; but, again, in numerical proportion the characters do not match exactly. During the comparison, a corresponding atmosphere of the supernatural and similar details of setting have been observed. Analogies have likewise appeared between the style and structure of the novel and these several accounts of the Overbury affair.

In view of the allusions to Overbury, Hawthorne's knowledge of the case, and this formidable sequence of parallels, a hypothetical explanation may now be given to the question that has been proposed: Could the Overbury materials have been Hawthorne's major immediate source for *The Scarlet Letter?* If so, what are the characteristics of Hawthorne's creative process that may explain the apparent differences between the sources and the novel? What are the probable steps in the genesis and evolution of the novel? And what new light may the sources throw on the meaning of the novel in relation to Hawthorne's art?

Between these coarse materials and the finished artistic product of the novel there is a wide difference. This discrepancy may be explained in part as the result of a rearrangement of materials which ignores the original chronology of events. Hester's imprisonment, punishment, and ostracism, for example, precede Chillingworth's revenge on Dimmesdale, whereas Lady Frances' similar situation followed Carr's revenge upon Overbury. The difference may be partially explained as the result of compression of materials. In the novel there are three major characters, whereas in the Overbury affair at least ten principal persons figure in the case. Motifs, which in the latter are apportioned among the ten, are in the novel integrated in three characters. The difference may be explained in part as the logical consequence of Hawthorne's making a single, unified narration out of a heterogeneous mixture of documents. Three of the main accounts of the case are themselves totally different. The prose tract is factual and tells the Overbury narration in historical context. The poem is imaginary, omits mention of the persons in the love triangle, takes up only five characters in the case, and interprets at least one of these, Anne Turner, with a sympathetic bias unique in the records. The trial proceedings are stale, matter-of-fact, and lacking in narrative order.

The difference may be explained partially as the result of a considerable amount of refinement of obscene and grotesque elements. The tawdry details of Lady Frances' witchcraft to gain Carr's love and induce frigidity in Essex may be said to have been omitted in Hawthorne's treatment of Hester's liaison with Dimmesdale. Only through subtle symbolism does Hawthorne relate her adultery to witchcraft. The grotesque blisters made by poisons on Overbury's body were refined into a symbolical hint of a painful, ghastly imprint of the letter A in Dimmesdale's breast. But the rumors of venereal disease ascribed to Overbury do not appear in the novel. Lady Frances' loathsome death caused by a diseased uterus, and said to be a divine punishment, is purged of these sordid facts in the lonely but serene death of Hester Prynne. The latter's divine punishment is that she has been disqualified by sin from achieving an improvement of woman's position.

The difference may be explained largely in terms of Hawthorne's previous writing experience. One of the many extremely important facts that Professor Randall Stewart has demonstrated is that the ingredients of the novel show not a marked difference from the preceding tales, but rather a decided similarity. The novel is indisputably a culmination, a reshaping, of his own literary materials.[1] The same themes and the same character types are to be found in the novel as in the tales. "Rappaccini's Daughter," for instance, represents a stage in Hawthorne's artistic development that seems, in some respects, preparatory for *The Scarlet Letter*. The character configuration—a beautiful woman, a young scholar, and an old man who experiments with poisons—anticipates the character arrangement of the love triangle in the novel.

114

The themes of isolation and of violation of the human soul foreshadow similar themes in the novel. To the artistic matrix that formed this tale may be added the elements of concealed sin from "The Minister's Black Veil," the supernatural atmosphere from "Young Goodman Brown," the Puritan New England setting from "The Gentle Boy," the style of popular legends and multiple rumors from "The Legends of the Province House," and it seems scarcely necessary—except for a new story outline—to theorize about a possible outside influence; the major ingredients in the novel seem to be evolved from the tales.

Yet, assuming that the Overbury materials crowded into Hawthorne's imagination in 1849, it is logical that they, too, would have been shaped into a form partaking of the substance of previous tales. The intellectual and artistic matrices that shaped earlier tales need not be expected to change because of a foreign admixture; they may be said, by the passing of time and other admixtures, merely to have been enlarged and made more receptive to new influences. Especially would this seem to be the case in the infiltration of new matter from the Overbury literature. Many elements in the affair seem to be suited to Hawthorne's peculiar artistic bias. Lady Frances' banishment, Forman's and Franklin's pseudo-science, Carr's deceitful violation of Overbury's soul, Helwyse's concealment of a secret sin, the narrator's gossipy style, Niccols' ghost story—these elements would appear to have been congenial to Hawthorne's genius. His mind could have readily assimilated and shaped them. They were not so new and different after all; he had been using materials such as these all his writing life. And as regards notions of adultery, of a woman punished on the scaffold in a special ornament of dress made by her, of the diabolizing effects of revenge upon one who indulges in it, and of a girl by the name of Pearl—elements stored up in Hawthorne's mind for use in future stories—the Overbury materials could have enabled him to realize these preconceived plans.

But a creative process of rearrangement, compression, combination, refinement, and organizing according to pre-established patterns of creative operation is not uncommon among artists. Nor

115

do these processes completely solve the problem of the differences between the Overbury materials and the novel; nor do they suggest any distinctive characteristic of Hawthorne's creative mind.

The greatest differences might possibly be explained as the result of a spiritualizing process of adaptation. That is, source elements entering Hawthorne's mind from the legal or physical plane emerged on a higher moral or spiritual plane. According to this explanation, Lady Frances' legal banishment was spiritualized into Hester's moral estrangement. Overbury's chemical poisoning was spiritualized into Dimmesdale's moral poisoning; not only does a spiritual canker pollute his entire moral system, but he inhales a poisonous atmosphere created by the secret malignity of Chillingworth's revenge. The vengeful murdering of Overbury's body was spiritualized into Chillingworth's attempted destruction of Dimmesdale's soul—or in Hawthorne's terms, the violation in cold blood of Dimmesdale's soul. Essex's sexual frigidity as regards his wife was spiritualized into Chillingworth's cold heart, lack of warm feelings toward humanity, and a depravity of soul. The human being Forman, who had people enter their names in his business directory, was adapted into the spiritual being of the Black Man, in whose book people sign away their souls. The vow of revenge made by Carr and Lady Frances, and the oath of secrecy shared by Lady Frances and Franklin, became transmuted into Chillingworth's spiritual bond with the Black Man. Helwyse's hanging, decreed by a legal tribunal, was spiritualized into Dimmesdale's death, brought about by God—or his conscience—who tortures him to repentance and leads him to a dying confession on the scaffold.

The spiritualizing process may also be illustrated by Hawthorne's adaptations of certain details into symbols of moral phenomena. Franklin's crooked shoulder and dark complexion were adapted in Chillingworth to symbolize a spiritual deformity. The spots on Overbury's body became, in the intimations of a mark upon Overbury's breast, the symbol of Dimmesdale's guilt and hidden sin. The witchcraft cabal of Lady Frances, Anne Turner, and Dr. Forman was adapted in the relationship between Hester, Mistress

116

Hibbins, and the Black Man to allegorize the sin of adultery, and,
by extension, Dimmesdale's lust and Chillingworth's revenge. The
character of Pearl likewise exemplifies Hawthorne's tendency to
allegorize spiritual phenomena. In the absence of much information about the daughter born in prison to Lady Frances, he re-
sorted to notes on his own daughter to bring to life in allegorical
fashion a mere factual skeleton of the girl Anne Carr.

This process of spiritualization of materials could not only
account for many of the most significant material changes that
took place between the Overbury story and the novel, but it
appears to be so fundamental to Hawthorne's creative processes
that it may well be one of the distinctive characteristics of his
artistic imagination. Perhaps he was not unaware of some such
trait of mind. In the preface to "Rappaccini's Daughter," he speaks
of an inveterate love of allegory which so refines his writings that
his plot and characters are apt to be invested "with the aspect of
scenery and people in the clouds." His writings, he says, must be
read from the proper point of view to bring them "within the
limits of our native earth."[2] He repeats these critical observations
in reverse in "Main Street." To a cantankerous spectator com-
plaining that the cardboard exhibitions create no illusion, Hawthorne, as showman, urges him to move his seat to where, with
the proper point of view, "the slips of pasteboard shall assume
spiritual life."[3] And in "The Custom House" he seems to char-
acterize the processes of his imaginative faculty as a spiritualization of material substance into things of the intellect. He compares
the way in which moonlight transforms into shadows the objects
in his room with the operation of the mind upon the shapes in
his imagination. Things real become changed into things spiritual
in what might be called a creative endeavor to reproduce the
"true and indestructible value that lay hidden" in ordinary life
(pp. 54-57). Future investigations of source changes may further
clarify the nature of Hawthorne's creative processes that seem to
be implied in these parallels between the Overbury materials and
The Scarlet Letter in the light of remarks scattered throughout
his works.

117

Part Six — Conclusion

Some possible principles of Hawthorne's creative procedure in transmuting the Overbury materials having been observed, the second concern is to frame a theory of the genesis and evolution of the novel implied in the foregoing chapters and consistent with the known facts. It is generally assumed that a story on the scarlet letter began to germinate in Hawthorne's mind about 1837, some twelve years before *The Scarlet Letter* was finished. For in that year he briefly described in "Endicott and the Red Cross" a beautiful woman wearing a red letter A sewed to her garment in token of her having committed adultery. Between 1837 and 1844 this vivid symbol seems to have become firmly implanted in his mind as possessing potentialities for a full-length tale. But apparently during these six years it did not gestate into more than an independent idea. For Hawthorne wrote in his notebooks in 1844 only a brief reminder to himself to write a tale on a woman who by the old colony law is doomed for life to wear the letter A sewed to her bosom for the crime of adultery. Not until six years later, that is, the early winter of 1849-1850, when James T. Fields was handed an incomplete manuscript of the story, was anything more heard of this story suggestion.[4] And on February 3, 1850, Hawthorne finished *The Scarlet Letter*.[5]

What happened between 1844 and 1849 to generate the static symbol into a novel? The evidence in the preceding chapters implies that, during the Custom House period or immediately afterwards, Hawthorne began to steep himself in the literature relating to the Overbury affair. It is likely that he was already familiar with its general outline. Perhaps he had previously been influenced by some of its details, as his use of the name *Jervase Helwyse* in "Lady Eleanor's Mantle" might suggest. Whatever may have been the magnetic force that attracted him to a study of its details at this time—whether Helwyse's concealment of a crime, Forman's magic, Carr's malicious revenge, the pervading sense of mystery, Lady Frances' adultery—he seems ultimately to have been influenced by them all in *The Scarlet Letter*. And he must not have been long in his perusal of the affair before the adulteresses, Lady Frances and Anne Turner, and the latter's infamous

118

badge—the starched yellow ruff which she was condemned to
wear at her death—became identified in his imagination with
the static symbol of the adulteress condemned to wear the letter
A for the rest of her natural life.

As soon as this identification took place, a story of the consequences of this marked woman's sin could have taken command
of the other materials on the affair. The static symbol became
vitalized. A surging flood of images from the Overbury affair
began to stream through his mind. Other dormant ideas were
aroused. Ideas and images floating loosely in his imagination
formed new chains of associations and were gathered up in the
general quickening activity of the creative processes.[6] The new
matter and the old, after becoming blended, began to be refined
and spiritualized, to be compressed, combined, and molded into
pre-established forms, and finally to be checked and rearranged
into a poetic order. The static symbol suggested by a harsh, ancient
law provided the idea for the story. But it was not a story in and
by itself. What kind of person could be made of this doomed
woman? How could she have been brought to her sin? In "Endicott and the Red Cross" Hawthorne had merely assigned her two
attributes: beauty and the art of needlework wherewith she might
embroider her own stigma. But would her child live? Who would
be her paramour? What kind of man should her husband be?
Or might he be dead? What could happen among this trio after
her sin became public? Before the symbol could have generated
a novel, these questions had need of answers. Possibly the Overbury materials provided most of this necessary groundwork of
a tale and inspired the evolvement of a fable for the narrative
treatment of this symbolic story idea.

A theoretical reconstruction of what might have taken place
in the determination of characters and the formation of plot has
been indicated by the parallels set out in Parts Three and Four
of this book. From the disconnected images crowding into Hawthorne's mind about the case of adultery and murder, there emerged
a love triangle. The character in the symbol became endowed with
the attributes of the two adulteresses, Lady Frances and Anne

Turner, women of a similar "disposition and temperature." For the newly formed creation, Hester, like them together, is young, beautiful, and possessed of the art of needlework. She is unhappily united in a marriage of convenience to a husband she does not love. And while he was absent, she had engaged in adultery with a young man of eminence in the social structure. In the same way, the parallels indicate that the attributes of the three husbands of the two women became indistinguishable in Hawthorne's mind and blended into an emerging husband. For when Chillingworth arrives, he finds his wife a sinner. A physician and a learned man, he is also a person of a frigid disposition. He cooly backs out of the picture and seeks to gain revenge on his marital interloper. In this revenging capacity, the husband gathered to himself the traits of the man who assisted Carr, Lady Frances' second husband, in his revenge. Thus, the husband in the evolving trio in Hawthorne's imagination became an old, swarthy-complexioned, crooked-shouldered man, an eager student of natural sciences, a kind of apothecary who dabbles in poisonous herbs, and a depraved villain.

Similarly, there collected around the figure of the third person in the new triangle the attributes of the paramour Carr: a man rising to eminence in matters of state and troubled with a guilty conscience. It appears that these attributes attracted similar traits from Overbury and Helwyse, and in the process brought with them the notions of Overbury's lingering death by poisoning and Helwyse's concealment of a sin. As this person in the triangle began to evolve upon American soil, a transition could have been made without great difficulty from the social and political eminence of Carr and Overbury to a minister at the head of the Puritan theocracy. Thus, both men in the new triangle, a physician and a minister, became men of superior status and intelligence. To equalize this high rank of the men, Hester correspondingly emerged as a person with a good family background, with a worthy feminine occupation, and with strong traits of thought as well as feeling. It was absolutely necessary to decide upon these characters before any sort of story could take shape. These elemental data about

120

the rudiments of a triangular situation, the evidence suggests, were supplied from accounts of the Overbury affair. (Making the characters intellectual and thoughtful is not only an original stroke but one that enables Hawthorne to make the serious themes of the novel more germane to the character analyses.)

Out of this tangled maze of plot motifs in the Overbury materials a narrative sequence could have begun to unfold in ordered succession. Hawthorne's task would have been to select and organize the images into place. The exact steps in the formulation of a plot are obscure. But three dominating influences could have been at work. First, Hawthorne's original plan called for a story of the life of a woman who wears the mark of her sin of adultery. It is consistent with his frame of mind that he should have elected to treat the story in terms of the consequences of this sin. The logic of probability in cases of adultery could have determined the arrangement of passions and conflicts. Concealment by the lover, revenge by the husband, and desire by the woman to avoid trouble by shielding the one and acquiescing, perhaps somewhat guiltily, to the other would appear to be rooted in human nature.

Nevertheless, as a second plot influence, the Overbury affair presented in a causal connection an outline containing just such elements as these used by Hawthorne: adultery, concealment, revenge, and ultimate punishment. Once Hawthorne's main story of the consequences of an act of adultery had taken command and had reduced all the characters to three within a triangular network of love and hate, the story evolved along a corresponding plotline of adultery, concealment, revenge, and punishment. A third controlling influence could have been the precise plot element of concealment or secrecy. Hawthorne's imagination seems to have seized upon this salient feature from the Overbury materials as the means of welding the other elements of revenge and poisoning into an organic plot structure. In accord with the original story suggestion, the novel thus begins with Hester's punishment on the scaffold some time after she has committed adultery, has been imprisoned, and has given birth to a child—details that attached themselves to the symbol from similar events surrounding Lady Frances' trial for murder. The initial situation consists of Hester's public disgrace in the market square before the Puritan tribunal. The lover's concealment and the husband's scheme of revenge had perhaps already presented themselves as possibilities for a plot. But focus first had to fall on Hester and the significance of the scarlet letter. The reactions of lover and husband had to be held back. The action is thus complicated by the husband's unexpected arrival and his decisions to conceal his identity and seek his wife's seducer. It is further complicated by the lover's failure to confess his guilt. It is triply complicated by Hester's refusal to name her guilty partner in the crime.

As a physician, Chillingworth is admitted to his wife's cell, where he makes her pledge an oath of secrecy regarding his identity. For since she will not disclose to him her paramour, he forces her to acquiesce in his secret plot to search out and gain revenge upon this unknown man. Hester's oath of secrecy—like Lady Frances'—and her consent to a plot of revenge—like Anne Turner's, according to Niccols—enables the other motifs in the narrative to develop. Dimmesdale's concealment of his sin causes his failing health. His sickness provides an opportunity for the physician-husband to become his medical adviser. The husband's concealment of his identity enables him to find cause to suspect spiritual disease at the base of the minister's sickness. A native sagacity finally enables Chillingworth to recognize Dimmesdale as the object of his search. Convinced of this fact, Chillingworth—like Carr upon Overbury—violates the sanctity of Dimmesdale's soul. By pretending to be his friend, he exerts a deleterious influence upon the minister, who is already being consumed by the corrosive poisons—like Overbury—of a secret guilt—like Helwyse.

The first climax in the story is reached when Hester renounces her oath of secrecy. First, she informs Chillingworth of her change of heart. Then she reveals to Dimmesdale her husband's identity and confesses—like the ghost of Anne Turner—her having consented to Chillingworth's vengeful plan of deception. The lovers plan to escape to Europe. But the poisons of secret guilt and hate have so debilitated Dimmesdale, who for seven years has been dying a lingering death, that he knows he has but little time to live. The main climax of the story is reached when Dimmesdale mounts the scaffold to confess publicly in a speech at his death—like Helwyse—the concealment of his guilt of sinning with Hester. In the denouement, Hester lives for a while in England, where Pearl is married, and then returns to work out in penitence the rest of her life in Boston. Dimmesdale is thus punished by a long illness of the soul and an ignominious, though triumphant, death. Chillingworth is punished by damnation. Hester is punished by her inability to become an apostle of a new order of marital relationship.

A possible explanation of how the persons of the sources could have contributed to the formation of a basic set of characters for the novel has been noticed as a necessary preliminary to the organization of the plot. Integration of these traits from different persons has also been cited as characteristic of Hawthorne's mind. The other general principles of Hawthorne's creative processes, namely, rearrangement, refinement, and spiritualization, may likewise explain the creation of characters. But each character seems to represent a slightly different mode of construction. In terms of the distinctive feature of Hawthorne's imagination, Dimmesdale may be the character most near a norm. Dimmesdale seems to be made chiefly by a process of spiritualizing Overbury's physical poisoning into a moral poisoning, with the moral motivation of concealed sin supplied from Helwyse. The result is a highly refined character. Pearl represents essentially the same type of character formation but with emphasis upon the allegorical. Chillingworth stands out as a thesis figure who conforms to the idea that revenge diabolizes a person. Possibly this archetypal formula by which he was constructed explains the transparent quality of his delineation.

In contrast to these techniques, Hester was perhaps developed by a more realistic standard. In constructing her, Hawthorne's moral imagination seems to have struck a happy balance with the primal facts received into his mind. By selecting, rearranging, purifying, and fusing details into an idealized creature, Hawthorne created in Hester Prynne his most individualized character. Strange as it appears, Mistress Hibbins is related in origin to Hester. Mistress Hibbins, as a simple witch, represents the appropriation of one of the figures of the sources, Anne Turner, without much modification. Yet, in view of the fact that Anne Turner is also a prototype of Hester, Mistress Hibbins demonstrates a capacity of Hawthorne's mind to keep the materials of his imagination flexible and thus to refashion and re-use them with different purposes. The Black Man may be regarded as a spiritualized portrait of Forman; or he may represent, along with Mistress Hibbins, Bellingham, Wilson, Eliot, and Winthrop, the reproduction of a character as nearly as possible to what he was in New England history. Finally, these types of character construction are not mutually exclusive. And with the exception of Eliot and Winthrop, all the characters are possibly composites of two or more persons, ennobled and idealized into fiction.

The Overbury materials throw little completely new light on the meaning of *The Scarlet Letter*. The novel is a self-sufficing artistic entity with its meaning embedded in its own structure. Yet, through analogy, certain elements seem to emerge more distinctly and contribute to the total meaning. Hawthorne's treatment of the salvation of the characters, by comparison with the views towards the souls of characters in the sources, points up his interpretations of the themes of the novel. Knowing the names of some probable prototypes of the characters affords an opportunity to examine the meaning of the names assigned to characters. The supernatural aspects of the Overbury materials give an insight into Hawthorne's use of the supernatural in the setting of the novel. And finally Hawthorne's style and structure, which appear to be well adapted to the presentation of a serious religious subject, clarify the relationship between the novel and "The Custom House."

As the static symbol began to accumulate mobile narrative force, it likewise became invested with thought and meaning. The central themes of the story seem to be ethical and religious: What is the nature of sin? and what is the effect of sin upon the salvation of the soul? Through the three major characters, Hawthorne presents three ramifications of each of these themes. All sin by nature seems to be invested with the character of doom (p. 253). Yet sin is of three degrees. Sin of passion, or of the flesh, is rooted in the human constitution. By sincere repentance and an open recognition of sin, as in the situation of Hester, it may result in moral elevation of a sinner's character. Sins rooted in nature are most harmful when by some scruple or principle of conscience they are allowed to remain hidden. Concealment of sin generates a poison that can destroy the moral sinews. For concealment may result, as in the case of Dimmesdale, in hypocrisy. Even when based upon sound religious rationalization, hypocrisy, a sin of principle, is a worse sin than one of the flesh. Worst of all, however, is the sin of cold, calculated purpose to deceive, betray, and plot against the soul of another person to achieve its damnation. Hatred and purposeful revenge upon the soul of an enemy are the New Testament equivalents of murder. Chillingworth's sin of violating Dimmesdale's soul deserves damnation. He whose heart is so cold as to perpetrate such a sin belongs to the order of Satan.

In the ambiguity of Hester's salvation, her character illustrates the essential complexity of the second theme: the consequences of sin upon the soul's salvation. Hester hopes, but she also doubts. Her open ignominy is in her favor, for it furthers her moral development. But she remains a frail woman, susceptible to sin, and incapable of performing any divine mission for womanhood. On the surface, Hawthorne seems to leave the question of her salvation ambiguous, but in fact he does not.

In Dimmesdale and Chillingworth, Calvinistic answers are also implied. A predestined soul, like Dimmesdale, is not immune to sin. But though he sins, he ultimately perseveres. Dimmesdale loses the assurance of his salvation. His moral system becomes poisoned. But finally his God-inspired conscience motivates him to do what is morally right. His confession, of which he should have long ago availed himself, clears away the clouds of despair, so that he can receive once again before entering Heaven the assurance of salvation. Upon a damned soul, like Chillingworth, the consequences of sin are to bring out his latent depravity. Why Chillingworth should have responded as he did is one of the mysterious truths of human nature. Yet it is not completely meaningless that Chillingworth seems doomed to evil. There exists an intelligible system of the universe, to which he himself refers his cold-hearted violation of Dimmesdale's soul and his incapacity to pardon the man who wronged him. He stolidly recognizes the intervention of a dark necessity in their lives, as a result of their first erring step. He, therefore, blames their tragedy on religious determinism (p. 210). *The Scarlet Letter* thus tells a story that gives expression for all time to the existence in man's nature of a moral conscience and to man's existence within a universe of spiritual dimensions.

In telling so universal a story, it seems appropriate that Hawthorne did not assign to his major characters the names of people in the Overbury affair or of people in New England history. He seems to have chosen names for their symbolical value. This art of name symbolism, in its own way, serves to maintain the universality of the lofty themes. The names of the background characters—Bellingham, Winthrop, Wilson, Eliot, and Hibbins—give the story a sense of geographical and historical reality. But the other names—Prynne, Hester, Chillingworth, Pearl, and Dimmesdale—lift the story out of the realm of pure history, so that Hawthorne can universalize this instance of human experience.

Two modes of name symbolism appear. One mode employs names that have a historical relevance but not a historical particularity. In naming Hester Prynne and Chillingworth, Hawthorne selected names that draw a parallel between these fictitious characters and historical persons. Their names provide a frame of historical reference which tells some special feature about them and their roles in the drama. Mistress Prynne's surname, by association with William Prynne, might suggest the type of disgraceful punishment that she undergoes, the scaffold of the pillory and the letter that is "branded" upon her. Hester's Christian name, by association with Esther, might relate to her concern with feminism. And Chillingworth's surname, by association with William Chillingworth, might suggest his intellectual cultivation and liberal rationalism. These names, therefore, provide a review of some of the intellectual high points related to the central themes, with which the novel is concerned: the concept of justice, the position of woman in the social structure, and the relative superiority of religious faith or rationalism.

The second mode of name symbolism has not been touched upon as yet. It is to employ a name to which an abstract meaning is directly attached without the aid of a historical referent. By means of an image expressed in the name and developed in the narration, Hawthorne allegorizes an attribute of character or a dramatic role. The method ranges from an obvious pun in Chillingworth's name and an apparent allegory in Pearl's name to the more subtle image patterns suggested in Dimmesdale's name.

Repeatedly, Hawthorne characterizes Chillingworth as cold and passionless. The scholar's heart is lonely and "chill" (p. 97); in "cold blood" he violates the sanctity of a human heart (p. 234). In the first half of Chillingworth's name Hawthorne puns on this characteristic of the frigid, depraved husband in a fashion reminiscent of the "humor" theory of naming characters, perhaps facetiously, by a dominant attribute—as, for instance, Henry Fielding's Mr. Allworthy.

Pearl's name is an example of that type of pure symbolism in the tradition of Spenser and Bunyan, in which a word or phrase typifies a moral condition. Hester named her child Pearl, "as being of great price,—purchased with all she had,—her mother's only treasure!" (P. 113.) She is the emblem of the great spiritual price that Hester paid for her sin, in shame, suffering, and spiritual torment. The pearl of great price scripturally, however, is salvation.[7] This second meaning is also brought out in the novel when Wilson tells Pearl that she must learn her catechism in order to wear in her bosom the "pearl of great price" (p. 138). Pearl may thus be taken as a dual symbol of the price of sin and also of the price of salvation. For Pearl is her mother's torture as well as her blessing; she is the embodiment of Hester's conscience which

127

reminds her of her transgression and therefore leads her to repentance (pp. 139, 144). At the expense of individuality in Pearl's character, Hawthorne still more intricately develops the character of Hester.

The use of the name *Dimmesdale* seems to be more original and less obtrusive allegory of the same type as *Pearl*. A subtle overtone of double meaning in the minister's name might suggest, in Bunyanesque fashion, the very essence of the effect of sin and hypocrisy upon Dimmesdale's moral character. *Dimmesdale* seems to be an allegorical abstraction of the minister's condition in terms of two images and the dramatic embodiment of one of them in the setting of the novel. First, the name typifies the dark moral wilderness through which Dimmesdale walks on account of his sin. Dimmesdale appears as "a being who felt himself quite astray and at a loss in the pathway of human existence, and could be at ease only in some seclusion of his own. Therefore, so far as his duties would permit, he trod in the shadowy by-paths" (p. 88). Life to him has become a dark affair lived out on a low and confused level. He might have climbed, says Hawthorne, to "the high mountain-peaks of faith and sanctity . . . had not the tendency been thwarted by the burden, whatever it might be, of crime or anguish, beneath which it was his doom to totter" (p. 173). Thus he is kept down "on a level with the lowest" and struggles along in a dim moral valley, confused, disorganized, and lost in the darkness of the black secret of his soul.

This image of the dim dale is dramatically embodied in the forest interview. The scene is symbolically placed in a "forest-dell" (p. 266) enveloped in "the dim medium of the forest-gloom" (p. 249). There in this "dim wood" (p. 228), a type of the moral wilderness, through which these sinners are laboring, Dimmesdale's abased moral force and the confusion of his spiritual being are intensified; by agreeing to elope, he succumbs to a temptation to commit again the sin which has darkened his soul for seven years. The "dim forest, with its little dell of solitude" (p. 285) is an apt emblem of Dimmesdale's character, as it is of the entire action that takes place between the lovers. This dim dale in the woods also represents the Valley of the Shadow of Death, through which Dimmesdale makes his pilgrimage on the way to the Celestial city. As his haggard figure approaches the shadow of the trees, his listless gait certifies a realization of the falsity of his life—it is "all emptiness!—all death!" (Pp. 226, 230.) A few days later, he has passed through the Valley and has reached the Heavenly City.

Interwoven in the texture of the novel is still another image which seems to relate to Dimmesdale's name. It applies to his consumptive wasting away. Hawthorne develops an image of the dimming of a lamp to indicate the minister's physical and moral decline. The "prospect that his dawning light would be extinguished" was imminent (p. 148). "What was he?" asks Hawthorne, "a substance?—or the dimmest of all shadows?" (P. 174.) By his hypocritical life, he has put himself in a false light and has become a shadow of his former self. The real substance of his character is fading into unreality and darkness. Dimmesdale fasts "in order to keep the grossness of this earthly state from clogging and obscuring his spiritual lamp" (p. 147); he fasts also as an act of penance and, possibly, as a means of rendering the body "a fitter medium of celestial illumination" (p. 174). With the conclusion of Dimmesdale's Election Sermon, the dimming lamp image vividly foreshadows his physical death and his rekindled spirituality. "The glow," writes Hawthorne, which the people "had just before beheld burning on his cheek, was extinguished, like a flame that sinks down hopelessly among the late-decaying embers" (p. 297). Many of the onlookers would not have been surprised to see this man, whom they thought a chosen holy light, ascending "before their eyes, waxing dimmer and brighter, and fading at last into the light of heaven" (p. 298).

The image of the dimming lamp is also employed in two scenes in which Dimmesdale shows himself true. On these occasions his spiritual lamp is surcharged and brightened. On the scaffold in the dim twilight, the shadowy figure of Dimmesdale takes the hands of Hester and Pearl into his own. Immediately a current of truth circulates through his system: "there came what seemed a tumultuous rush of new life, other life than his own, pouring like a torrent into his heart, and hurrying through all his veins, as if the mother and the child were communicating their vital warmth to his half-torpid system. The three formed an electric chain" (pp. 185-186). A moment later, a meteoric light gleams far through the sky, showing him, in its brightness, standing with his guilty partner. In the forest, when Dimmesdale hears Hester's plans for them to live a true life, a fitful light flashes up in the minister's eyes and dies away (p. 238). The whole dimness of the forest gloom is dispelled when Hester removes the scarlet letter from her bosom. Truth and love momentarily effect this transfiguration.

The figurative connotations of the names *Chillingworth, Pearl,* and *Dimmesdale* thus seem to take the reader symbolically into complex nuances of human experience as examined in the novel: the cold heart, the pricelessness of human salvation, and the spiritual darkness that comes with hypocrisy and the loss of the assurance of salvation.

The religious and ethical themes of the novel are also maintained in the Boston setting of Puritan New England. The worldly paraphernalia of most consequence to the drama are themselves physical symbols of a religious faith and an ethical code: the meeting house, the prison, and the scaffold. Central to the story, as these items of setting perhaps were in New England life, it matters little if they may have been sharpened in Hawthorne's imagination by the English counterparts of Westminster Hall, the Tower of London, and the scaffold on Tower Hill. Similarly, the gallery at Westminster Hall, the forum at Guildhall, and Loseley Hall at Surrey, England, if adapted by Hawthorne, were made indigenous to the worldly locus of Boston. Their use, in the gallery appended to the meeting house, in the market-place, and in Bellingham's hall, enlarges and makes more vivid Hawthorne's portrayal of the New England scene where the action in the natural sphere takes place.

But in accord with the religious and ethical issues embodied in the characters, Hawthorne expands the setting into a macrocosm reflecting universally the spiritual drama in their souls. In another context, Hawthorne labels his characteristic genre of expression a "psychological romance." He stipulates that the subjects of his stories originate in the dusky region of "the depths of our common nature." He proposes to present life in a "slightly idealized and artistic guise."[8] In *The Scarlet Letter* he demonstrates this creed. He externalizes the affairs of the soul—human depravity, the resulting internal passions, and the soul's salvation—in a spiritual by-plot. This auxiliary plot may be regarded as an allegory of sin, as a supernatural motivation integral to the main action, or as a universal drama itself in which the characters of the novel play roles subsidiary to those of the leading protagonists, God and Satan. Whatever critical designation it may go by, this spiritual activity seems to fall within the province of setting atmospherically developed.

The action of this allegorical by-plot takes place in a universe that knows no boundaries between the natural and the spiritual worlds. It begins, as does the main story, when Hester and Dimmesdale momentarily forget God (p. 304). Through Mistress Hibbins' arrangements, Hester holds an interview with the Black Man (pp. 222-223), and, as some people later claim, by him she has a child (p. 124). At any rate, he seems to have gained for her the object of her desire, Dimmesdale's love, and from the fires of his altar in hell he brands both Hester and Dimmesdale with a mark of their meeting with him. When Chillingworth arrives in the colony and finds his wife a sinner, he betakes himself to the Black Man and makes a bond (p. 100). He signs away his soul in exchange for revenge upon the seducer of his wife. The Black Man assigns him fiends to use (p. 171) and allows him the use of hell-fire in his laboratory (p. 156). With this superhuman assistance, Chillingworth soon discovers by the mark on Dimmesdale that this man is his wife's lover (p. 169). According to the terms of the bond with his master, Chillingworth tortures Dimmesdale's conscience. After her release from prison, Hester is tempted by Satan to remain in Boston to be near Dimmesdale (pp. 103-104). Hester, however, will not visit the Black Man any more, even though Mistress Hibbins makes the arrangements and

131

tells her about witch meetings (p. 144). Seven years later, after the forest meeting between Dimmesdale and Hester, Dimmesdale is so confused that he does not even remember whether he met the Black Man there and signed away his soul (pp. 263-265).

For the most part God remains an inactive participant. According to some spectators, He brings Chillingworth to Dimmesdale's door (pp. 148-149). Some also think He has permitted Chillingworth's torture upon Dimmesdale (p. 156). But by an inauspicious hieroglyphic in the sky one night, He makes his presence visibly known. He signifies through the letter A that Dimmesdale is guilty —a sign which the people, however, interpret to stand for Angel, in honor of Winthrop's death the same night (p. 192). When Hester and Dimmesdale make plans to escape and Hester discards the letter, God joins in the action more directly. As Fate, He picks up the letter and hands it back to Hester (p. 253). On Election Day, He does not permit the lovers to escape as they had planned (p. 285). He leads Dimmesdale to complete repentance and to a dying confession upon the scaffold (pp. 299-300, 304). And when some time later Chillingworth dies, God permits Chillingworth to fulfill the terms of his bond with the Black Man. Chillingworth thus delivers his soul to his master (p. 307).

Sin, Hawthorne seems to be saying, is an absolute spiritual force. It proceeds from the soul of man, but it originates in the principle of Evil, personalized in Christianity as Satan, the Adversary of God. Through this traditional supernatural fable, Hawthorne dramatically allegorizes sin, predestination, and damnation.

Hawthorne's atmospheric treatment of setting, expressing deep-seated spiritual truths and longings, is not to be confined in genesis to any primary source of the novel, in spite of an abundance of hints in the Overbury materials about witchcraft. The treatment is in the tradition of the Hellenic-Hebraic stream of literature. Homer, Dante, Shakespeare, Milton, Bunyan, and Goethe established a legacy in poetry and prose allegory which Hawthorne inherited. Like his predecessors, Hawthorne recreated the universal background of his character's culture and their beliefs in the spiritual world around them to produce not only a high species of supernatural realism but also a vehicle for allegorizing man's sinful soul.

The style of the novel further contributes to the exalted themes. Solemn and dignified sentences move the narrative along at a gravely slow pace. The learned diction creates a somber mood. The imagery is organic to the story. Cross-references of diction, imagery, names, or allusions make for a compact tale in which scarcely a word seems isolated from some other aspect of the story. To give a sense of authority in re-creating the supernatural background, as well as to elaborate less obtrusively on the themes, Hawthorne adopts the style of an editor. He pretends that the story is the work of an antiquarian who drew it up from oral testimony. Hawthorne is thus able to reproduce as their own the beliefs and traditions of the people and to add to the serious narration the wisdom of an objective narrator. In the use of this stylistic device a new sense of the unity of "The Custom House," the novel, and the conclusion seems to be implied. First, by analogy with the editorial structure of *The Narrative History*, the basis of oral testimony of "The Five Years," and the visitation by a ghost in Richard Niccols' "Sir Thomas Overbury's Vision," the structural framework of the novel more clearly emerges. Second, the editorial ruse of "The Custom House" is consistently maintained in the novel, and an explicit reference is made to the edited manuscript in the final chapter.

Third, on the basis of mood, "The Custom House" introduction has a right to claim a unity of a sort with the novel. Though often regarded as a superfluous appendage to the novel, "The Custom House" should perhaps be viewed as a necessary vestibule. Hawthorne himself designated it an entrance hall.[9] It was originally written, he says, to introduce a volume of tales. Believing most of them, and especially *The Scarlet Letter*, to consist of gloomy passages that would discourage the reader and give a wrong impression of the author, he conceived "The Custom House" as a means of dispelling some of the gloom (p. 64). This serio-comic style, in which "The Custom House" with its Custom House portraits is written, is a fitting entrance hall to the somber, gloomy, edifice of the novel. The sketch leads up gradually to the appropriate mood. The mystery enshrouding the scarlet letter and the grim exhortation of Pue's ghost contribute to establishing a mood of humorous sobriety which loses its humor in the opening lines of the novel but retains and intensifies its solemnity. Similarly, in view of the over-all structural purpose, the concluding chapter, which ties up loose narrative ends and refers again to Pue's manuscript, is actually a rear annex to conduct the reader out of the main edifice. As the introduction leads emotionally into the story, the conclusion affords a gradual relaxation of emotional tension after the tumultuous climax of the last scene. The conclusion thus unites "The Custom House" and *The Scarlet Letter* into an aesthetic whole.

Finally, this analysis of Hawthorne's allusions to the murder of Sir Thomas Overbury has brought to light materials which present a solid claim to recognition as important sources of *The Scarlet Letter*. The numerous parallels between the novel and accounts of the murder indicate not a mere chance borrowing of a few details, but a major creative operation that assimilated a group of materials into a new and vastly superior poetic arrangement. A study of the parallels reveals at work a distinctively original mode of transmutation by which source materials were elevated from a physical to a spiritual level of treatment. The source materials instructively point up by analogy many obscure patterns in the design of the novel and provide, it seems, commentary on both its form and content. The evidence warrants a fairly certain conclusion that these accounts of the Overbury murder were the major sources which possessed Hawthorne's imagination and enabled him to energize the static symbol of a woman wearing a letter A into the dynamic narration of *The Scarlet Letter*. Yet this knowledge in no way detracts from the originality of Hawthorne's creative power nor from the sublimity of the novel. More than ever, Hawthorne demonstrates his indisputable kinship with the great literary artists. Out of these tawdry materials relating to an ancient crime he created in *The Scarlet Letter* one of the imperishable masterpieces of world literature.

NOTES

CHAPTER 1

1. Throughout, I avoid trying to solve the mystery of Overbury's murder. Modern interpretations of the facts have been made by Sidney Lee and Samuel R. Gardiner in their lives of Overbury and Carr, respectively, in *The Dictionary of National Biography*—hereafter cited as *DNB*; by Edward F. Rimbault, *The Miscellaneous Works . . . of Sir Thomas Overbury* (London, 1856); by James Maidment, *Sir Thomas Overbury's Vision* (Hunterian Club, No. XVII, Glasgow, 1873). The best of the older accounts, for its lively imaginative touches, is by S. R. Gardiner, *The History of England, 1603-1642* (Boston, 1883), II, 166-187, 331-363. The most recent study available for this work is by Edward Abbot Parry, *The Overbury Mystery: A Chronicle of Fact and Drama of the Law* (New York, 1925). Recognizing that the evidence had been tampered with, Parry decided to write the "romance of the story without calling it history" (p. 11). Hawthorne would have agreed with him that the case was a "first-rate" story, "an unsolved mystery, founded on rumors of adultery, murder, and witchcraft" and having "the romance of a beautiful woman as the base of it" (pp. 7, 17). The most authoritative study yet made, exploring the crime and all its political and social implications, is by W. L. McElwee, *The Murder of Sir Thomas Overbury* (New York, 1952), which appeared too late to guide me.

2. According to Marion L. Kesselring, *Hawthorne's Reading, 1828-1850 . . . Salem Athenaeum* (New York Public Library, 1949), p. 52, Hawthorne knew and used a selected edition of *The Miscellany* (London, 1793). This edition contains only the prose tract; both the poem and the tract appear in the larger collections of 1744 and 1808, which would have been available in near-by Boston. All references to Hawthorne's reading are based on Kesselring's compilation, unless otherwise stated.

3. James T. Fields, *Yesterdays with Authors* (Boston, 1900), pp. 62-63.

4. Randall Stewart, "Recollections of Hawthorne by His Sister Elizabeth," *American Literature*, XVI (January, 1945), p. 324.

5. Horatio Bridge, *Personal Recollections of Nathaniel Hawthorne* (New York, 1893), pp. 110-112.

6. George Sherburn in *A Literary History of England*, ed. Albert C. Baugh (New York, 1948), p. 1087.

7. Nathaniel Hawthorne, *The Complete Works of Nathaniel Hawthorne* (Riverside Edition), ed. George Parsons Lathrop (Boston, 1890), XII, 446 and VII, 498—hereafter cited as *Works*. I have not yet been able to satisfy myself whether the Elwes of the Overbury crime was related to the Elwes in the Hawthorne family and thus a very distant relative of Hawthorne himself. Also, the reader will have noticed by now the variant spellings of this name and that I have chosen to use the form "Jervase Helwyse," in accord with Hawthorne's practice in "Lady Eleanor's Mantle." Hawthorne himself uses different spellings for the

135

given name: "Jervase" and "Gervase," which we have seen, and in "The Christmas Banquet" and *The House of the Seven Gables* he has a "Gervayse Hastings" and a "Gervayse Pyncheon," respectively. In the Overbury records, both given name and surname appear in many different forms, including "Gervais Helwys," "Jervis Elwes," "Jervays Elvys," "Jervace Helwisse," "Gervase Helwise," "Elwaies," "Elwayes," and "Yelvis." See Andrew Amos, *The Great Oyer of Poisoning* (London, 1846), p. 45.

8. Lucy Aikin, *Memoirs of the Court of King James the First* (London, 1822), II, 23.

9. Quoted in Frank P. Stearns, *The Life and Genius of Nathaniel Hawthorne* (Boston, 1906), p. 221.

10. *Works*, I, 487.

11. Randall Stewart, *The American Notebooks by Nathaniel Hawthorne* (New Haven, 1933), p. 107.

12. *The Road to Xanadu: A Study in the Ways of the Imagination* (Boston, 1927).

CHAPTER 2

1. Michael Sparke, *The Narrative History of King James, for the First Fourteen Years* (London, 1651), pp. 15, 17, 21—hereafter cited as *NH*. This volume includes "The Five Years of King James," a principal source of Hawthorne's knowledge of the affair, and also "Truth Brought to Light by Time," which duplicates material on the trials of the accomplices in the *State Trials*. Because of the wider scope of *NH*, and its easier accessibility to me, my references to the tract and many to the trial reports are to it. The work is reproduced in *Somers Tracts*, ed. Sir Walter Scott (London, 1809), II, 262-363.

2. *NH*, p. 114.

3. *NH*, p. 31.

4. *NH*, p. 135.

5. *NH*, p. 13.

6. Richard Niccols, "Sir Thomas Overbury's Vision," *The Harleian Miscellany* (London, 1808-1811), III, 344-345—hereafter cited as *HM*.

7. *NH*, p. 70.

8. *A Complete Collection of State Trials and Proceedings for High Treason and Other Crimes and Misdemeanors from the Earliest Period to the Year 1783*, compiled by Thomas Bayly Howell (London, 1816), II, 956—hereafter cited as *State Trials*.

9. *NH*, p. 71.

10. *State Trials*, II, 953.

11. *Ibid.*, 954.

12. Thomas Birch, *The Court and Times of James the First* (London, 1849), I, 407.

13. *NH*, p. 141.

14. *State Trials*, II, 954.

15. *HM*, III, 357, 359.

16. *NH*, p. 137.

17. Alfred John Kempe, *The Loseley Manuscripts* (London, 1836), p. 383.

18. Andrew Amos, *The Great Oyer of Poisoning* (London, 1846), p. 21.

19. Amos, p. 437; *The Works of Francis Bacon, Lord Chancellor of England*, ed. Basil Montague (Philadelphia, 1842), II, 518-519.

20. *State Trials*, II, 957-961.

21. *State Trials*, II, 957.

22. For this perversion of justice, King James and his Court have been severely castigated by later historians. If any one was culpable in the murder of Overbury, it was the Countess. See Birch, I, 407, 419; Amos, p. 21; Gardiner, II, 361.

23. *NH*, pp. 179-180.

24. Birch, I, 404.

25. Kempe, p. 400. An entry in the *Calendar of State Papers, Domestic Series, of the Reign of James I, 1611-1618*, ed. Mary Everett Green (London,

1858), for Nov. 11, 1615, states: "The Countess intends not to be hanged, but to die in child-bed." Another entry, Nov. 26, says that the King appointed midwives to be "answerable that she does not miscarry, either by her own wilfulness, or by the malice of any other." This work came out after Hawthorne's novel, but the entries may have been available elsewhere.

26. Kempe, p. 400.
27. Birch, I, 422.
28. *NH*, pp. 174-175.
29. *State Trials*, II, 961.
30. *State Trials*, II, 989.
31. *HM*, III, 355.

32. *HM*, III, 360.
33. Compare Wakefield in "Wakefield," *Works*, I, 153; Beatrice in "Rappaccini's Daughter," *Works*, II, 130; Ethan Brand in "Ethan Brand," *Works*, III, 495.
34. *NH*, p. 186.
35. *HM*, VI, 9.
36. Kempe, p. 395.
37. Kempe, p. 397.
38. Kempe, p. 383.
39. Birch, I, 395-396.
40. Birch, I, 409.
41. John Oldmixon, *The History of England, during the Reigns of the Royal House of Stuart* (London, 1730), p. 44.

CHAPTER 3

1. *NH*, pp. 11-12, 170.
2. *NH*, p. 170.
3. *NH*, pp. 11-12.
4. *NH*, pp. 14-15.
5. *NH*, p. 57.
6. *NH*, p. 46.
7. *NH*, p. 166.
8. *State Trials*, II, 963.
9. *NH*, p. 117.
10. *NH*, p. 48.
11. *NH*, p. 158.
12. *NH*, pp. 48-49, 52.
13. *HM*, III, 349.
14. *NH*, p. 44.
15. *HM*, III, 366.
16. *NH*, p. 49.
17. *NH*, p. 15.
18. *NH*, p. 44.
19. *HM*, III, 366.
20. *HM*, III, 349.

21. *NH*, p. 166.
22. *HM*, III, 363.
23. *HM*, III, 361-362.
24. Amos, pp. 21-22.
25. *NH*, p. 149.
26. *HM*, III, 355, 360.
27. *NH*, pp. 30-31.
28. Kempe, p. 390.
29. Birch, I, 284.
30. Amos, p. 7. Arthur Wilson—*The History of Great Britain* (London, 1653), p. 64—makes a statement concerning Princess Elizabeth at her marriage in 1612 that confirms this item of ceremonial etiquette: "Her Vestments were White, the Emblem of Innocency; her hair dishevel'd, hanging down her back at length, an Ornament of Virginity."

CHAPTER 4

1. *NH*, pp. 150-151.
2. *NH*, pp. 151-152.
3. *NH*, pp. 152-153.
4. *NH*, p. 156.
5. *State Trials*, II, 983.
6. *NH*, pp. 187-188.
7. *State Trials*, II, 966; *NH*, p. 188;

Amos, p. 27.
8. *State Trials*, II, 1020.
9. Sir Anthony Weldon, *The Court and Character of King James* (London, 1651), p. 113; Kempe, p. 395.
10. "Overbury"; Wilson, p. 83.
11. Kempe, p. 395.

CHAPTER 5

1. Professor Randall Stewart has demonstrated this characteristic of Hawthorne's imagination whereby several traits from different persons are assimilated into one character. The clearest example is perhaps that of Dimmesdale who comprehends from Reuben Bourne in "Roger Malvin's Burial" the idea of concealment, "from the Reverend Mr. Hooper ["The Minister's Black Veil"] certain concomitants of the role of clergyman, and from Roderick Elliston ["Egotism: or, the Bosom Serpent"] a characteristic gesture"—*The American Notebooks by Nathaniel Hawthorne* (New Haven, 1933), p. lxvi. Though this example applies only to materials in his own tales, the same method of cumulative assimilation seems to have been employed with respect to the persons in the sources presented in this study.

2. Kempe, p. 409.
3. Robert Codrington, "The Life and Death of the Illustrious Robert, Earl of Essex," *HM*, VI, 9.
4. *HM*, III, 357.
5. *NH*, "Epistle to Reader."
6. *HM*, III, 357.
7. *HM*, III, 357.
8. *NH*, p. 9.
9. *HM*, III, 357.
10. *NH*, pp. 12-13, 15.
11. *NH*, pp. 15-16, 19-20.
12. *NH*, p. 68.
13. Kempe, p. 384.

14. *HM*, III, 359.
15. *NH*, p. 13.
16. *Biographia Britannica*, "Devereux"; *NH*, p. 9.
17. *NH*, pp. 19-20.
18. *NH*, pp. 30, 79-107; *State Trials*, II, 785-862.
19. *NH*, p. 141.
20. *HM*, III, 360.
21. *HM*, III, 355, 360.
22. *State Trials*, II, 929.
23. Amos, p. 223.
24. *HM*, III, 360.

CHAPTER 6

1. *NH*, p. 8.
2. *NH*, pp. 14-15.
3. *NH*, p. 46.
4. *NH*, pp. 54, 23, 18.
5. *HM*, III, 347.
6. *NH*, pp. 54-55.

7. *HM*, III, 347.
8. *NH*, p. 54.
9. *NH*, p. 126.
10. *NH*, p. 117.
11. *HM*, III, 351.

12. There may be difference of opinion regarding this interpretation of Dimmesdale's character. Some critics concede no repentance to Dimmesdale until this final scene. The view that I have taken gives Dimmesdale not only the advantage of genuine repentance but shows him saved from the beginning of the novel, in accordance with the Calvinistic doctrine of Predestination, a dogma which Dimmesdale, as a Puritan divine, may be said to have held. (A counterpart to this dogma will appear in Chillingworth's Reprobation.) But this view raises a debatable question: If Dimmesdale is truly saved, why does he not confess sooner? Since I have not met previously with the above interpretation, I shall anticipate my own question with a suggestion that an answer may lie in Dimmesdale's religious zeal. Hawthorne has shown him in a moral conflict, in a tragic dilemma. Should he confess to regain peace? or should he conceal his sin and continue to perform his calling by working in behalf of the spiritual welfare of his parishioners? Dimmesdale poses his own problem in conversation with Chillingworth: guilty as one may be, he asks, may he not, neverthe-

less, retain "a zeal for God's glory and man's welfare" and shrink from displaying himself sinful before men? (P. 162.) Thus he allows concern for his reputation and the injury its blemish may do to his spiritual influence interfere with his own soul's health. For paradoxically, in this case, he puts what he deems to be God's will first, and it fails him. Hawthorne shows, therefore, the folly of Dimmesdale's decision to conceal his sin and carry on with religious work while suffering from a spiritual canker. His choice not only leads to hypocrisy but to moral and, ultimately, physical decay. In spite of a divine mercy that at birth makes pure the spiritual roots of some persons—from the Calvinistic viewpoint—man, implies Hawthorne, must be true before men. A parallel with Dimmesdale's dilemma, composed of a social versus a religious horn, has been seen in the conflict of Helwyse, as interpreted by Niccols. Bacon's characterization of Helwyse, as a man who "lacked rather fortitude than honesty" (*State Trials*, II, 955) might also apply to Dimmesdale as he decides his complex problem. Though honest in his striving to do the will of God, Dimmesdale lacks social fortitude and thus enters upon a career of hypocrisy until the moment of his death. Honesty with God is not enough for spiritual health, according to Hawthorne. Human nature demands social honesty as well.

13. *NH*, p. 156.

14. "The Lieutenant of the Tower's Speech and Repentance, at the Time of His Death," *HM*, III, 321.

15. *HM*, III, 322.

16. *HM*, III, 364.

17. *HM*, III, 349.

18. *HM*, III, 351.

Chapter 7

1. These two men are similar also in possessing, or being charged with a frigid disposition. Despite his wife's accusations, however, Essex seems to have been a warm and affectionate husband (Kempe, p. 383; *NH*, p. 9). But the mere association of frigidity with Essex could have acted as a stimulus to Hawthorne's imagination, for he appears to have had a lifelong preoccupation with men who were frigid by nature. Rappaccini, Ethan Brand, Richard Digby in "The Man of Adamant," and Gervayse Hastings in "The Christmas Banquet," all possessed cold hearts ahead of Chillingworth.

2. In the narratives of the Overbury case there are mentioned, besides Mistress Turner's physician-husband, also Forman, Franklin, Marvin (Mayerne?), de la Belle, and Weston, all of whom were physicians or served in that capacity.

3. *NH*, pp. 43-44.

4. *HM*, III, 352.

5. *NH*, p. 44.

6. *NH*, pp. 38, 138.

7. *NH*, pp. 138-139.

8. *HM*, III, 365.

9. *HM*, III, 365.

10. *HM*, III, 366.

11. *HM*, III, 364.

12. *HM*, III, 364.

13. *HM*, III, 367.

14. *NH*, p. 139.

15. Chillingworth's degeneration into a fiend through the course of his revenge recalls a note Hawthorne recorded in his journal on November 17, 1847, to write "a story of the effects of revenge, in diabolizing him who indulges in it" (Stewart, p. 121). Chillingworth's two closest counterparts, Carr and Franklin, could have fulfilled this story hint. By avenging himself on Overbury, Carr's seemingly warm and friendly nature degenerated into a mortal malice; possessed by a fiend, as Niccols pictures him, Franklin represents a man already diabolized.

16. Stewart, pp. 198-200, 205, 210-211.
18. Stewart, pp. 210-211.
17. Stewart, p. 201.
19. Stewart, p. 200.

CHAPTER 8

1. *NH*, pp. 12-13.
2. *NH*, pp. 15-16.
3. *NH*, p. 68.
4. *NH*, pp. 137-138.
5. *NH*, pp. 140-141.
6. *NH*, p. 140.

7. John Nichols, *The Progresses, Processions, and Magnificent Festivities, of King James the First* (London, 1828), III, 120. Mistress Hibbins—comparable to other real personages who figure in the novel, for instance, Governor Bellingham and John Wilson—is the name of a woman who actually lived in Boston and was executed for witchcraft. Joseph Barlow Felt—*The Annals of Salem* (Salem, 1827), p. 192—records that in 1656, at a session of the General Court at Boston, with William Hathorne as Deputy, "They condemn Ann Hibbins, of Boston, widow of the Agent in England, to be executed as a witch, on the 19th of June." Hawthorne's use of this name for a witch who parallels Anne Turner may not have been unpremeditated. Notice the similarities between these two women: both were named Anne, both were widows, and both were executed for witchcraft.

8. *NH*, "Epistle To Reader." Mistress Hibbins of *The Scarlet Letter* is not the only fictional character who learned from Mistress Turner the secret of the yellow starch. One of Hawthorne's favorite authors, Sir Walter Scott, portrays another protégée of this woman in *The Fortunes of Nigel—The Waverley Novels,* Portrait Edition (London, 1913), XIV, 88, 98. Describing Dame Ursula, Scott writes: "She had been a pupil of Mrs. Turner, and learned from her the secret of making the yellow starch, and it may be, two or three other secrets of more consequence, though perhaps none that went to the criminal extent of those whereof her mistress was accused." Further on, Dame Ursula herself alludes to her teacher: "I shall never forget poor Mistress Turner, my honored patroness, peace be with her! She had the ill-luck to meddle in the matter of Somerset and Overbury, and so the great earl and his lady slipt their necks out of the collar, and left her with some half dozen others to suffer in their stead. I shall never forget the sight of her standing on the scaffold with the ruff round her pretty neck, all done up with the yellow starch which I had so often helped her to make, and that was soon to give place to a rough hempen cord."

9. Cotton Mather, *The Wonders of The Invisible World,* ed. John Offer (London, 1862), pp. 30, 81, 169.

10. To my knowledge, only twice does Hawthorne allude to the Devil as the Black Man before *The Scarlet Letter,* and only once afterwards. These allusions occur in "The Prophetic Pictures," in "Main Street," and in "Feathertop: A Moralized Legend." But neither context includes the details of entering names in his book in a formal witchcraft compact. Nor is this curious book in "A Virtuoso's Collection," where we might expect among this universal assortment of oddities to find it mentioned. Here are Cornelius Agrippa's iron-clasped book of magic and the "blood-encrusted pen with which Faust signed away his salvation," but not the Black Man's book.

11. *NH*, pp. 20-21.
12. *NH*, p. 137.
13. *NH*, pp. 104-105.
14. *NH*, p. 140.
15. *HM*, III, 359.
16. Kempe, p. 388.
17. *State Trials*, II, 951; Sir Anthony

Notes — Chapter 9

Weldon, *The Court and Character of King James the First* (London, 1653), pp. 109-111.

18. *NH*, pp. 138-139; Amos, p. 16.

19. The title Black Man for the Devil does not appear in the documents specifically reporting the Overbury case. But in the *State Trials* this title is mentioned in a case following the Overbury trials. Mary Smith, in "The Case of Mary Smith, for Witchcraft," testifies that the Devil "appeared unto her . . . in the shape of a blacke man, . . . and . . . they entered tearmes of a compact, he requiring that she should forsake God, and depend upon him" (II, 1049-1051).

CHAPTER 9

1. This seven-year period that the story covers coincides with the prison term served by Carr and Lady Frances, who were taken into custody in the autumn of 1615 and were released in January, 1622. But in the material surrounding, though not a part of, the Overbury affair, appear two other details that also point up the seven-year interim in a story of adultery and revenge. One detail occurs in a passage in *The Harleian Miscellany* in a "Letter to a Member of Parliament" (1675), containing reasons why a law should be passed to punish adultery with death. The author cites as a precedent for greater severity a ruling by the Ancyran Council, in A.D. 315, which "ordains seven years penance for it" (*HM*, VIII, 69). The second detail occurs in Weldon's *Court and Character* and involves the Earl of Northampton, Lady Frances' great uncle and the friend of Robert Carr. Northampton, who hated Sir Robert Mansell, once said: "Body of God, I will be content to be damned perpetually in Hell, to be revenged of that proud Welshman; and did so hate him, that he kept an Inquisition on him seven years" (p. 20). Embracing themes of revenge and adultery common to the novel, these passages may be revealing. Moreover, Northampton's oath of revenge with a clause that he will gladly accept damnation recalls the circumstances of Chillingworth's oath and damnation. Northampton has also been compared already on two points to Chillingworth (Chapter III). E. C. Ross—"A Note on *The Scarlet Letter*," *Modern Language Notes*, XXXVII (January, 1922), pp. 58-59—has suggested that seven years may be related to the religious theme, the breaking of the seventh commandment. Certainly, the mystic and religious overtones of the number *seven* are of the utmost importance, regardless of any immediate reminder of the number.

2. *HM*, III, 352.
3. Kempe, p. ix.
4. Kempe, p. xiv.
5. Kempe, pp. xv-xvi.
6. Hawthorne discusses this subject in "The Custom House" (*Works*, V, 55-57), "Preface" to the second edition of *Twice-Told Tales* (*Works*, I, 16), "Rappaccini's Daughter" (*Works*, II, 107-108), and the prefaces to *The House of the Seven Gables* (*Works*, III, 13-16), *The Blithedale Romance* (*Works*, V, 321-323), and *The Marble Faun* (*Works*, VI, 13-17). He illustrates this principle of composition in "Young Goodman Brown," "The Gray Champion," *The House of the Seven Gables*, and many other works besides *The Scarlet Letter*.

7. Kempe, pp. 381-382.
8. Kempe, p. 387.
9. *HM*, III, 364, 367.
10. *HM*, III, 357.
11. *HM*, III, 349, 351, 364.
12. *NH*, pp. 15-16; Kempe, pp. 382, 387-389.
13. *NH*, pp. 20-21, 137.
14. *NH*, pp. 104-105.

141

Notes — Chapter 10

CHAPTER 10

1. *Works*, I, 487, 303.

2. At least once, the court secretary who recorded the proceedings also uses the word: Weston confessed that the murderers were not insensible to "how ignominiously they buryed" Overbury (*NH*, p. 126). See also HM, III, 345.

3. *NH*, p. 55.

4. *NH*, p. 57.

5. *NH*, p. 42.

6. *NH*, p. 166.

7. *NH*, p. 153.

8. *NH*, p. 156.

9. *NH*, pp. 135, 160; *State Trials*, II, 968.

10. *NH*, p. 153.

11. *NH*, p. 157.

12. Hawthorne's two allusions to Anne Hutchinson (pp. 68, 199) illustrate how an allusion to a New England personage contributes to the novel. By citing Anne Hutchinson in comparison with Hester, Hawthorne draws attention to aspects of Hester's character. Like Hester, Anne was imprisoned and banished; she was also urged by Reverend John Wilson to confess her errors; she similarly gave cause to be suspected of witchcraft. A sturdy individualist and an unorthodox thinker, she was thought by many people to be a prophetess, as Hester vainly imagines she herself might become (p. 311). Moreover, since the two figures would have been contemporaries, the allusion demonstrates a fidelity to both the history and spirit of the times. See Hawthorne's "Mrs. Hutchinson" in *Works*, XII, 217-226, and John Winthrop, *Journal* (Original Narratives of Early American History), ed. James Kendall Hosmer (New York, 1908), I, 243-252; II, 8.

13. *NH*, p. 108.

14. *State Trials*, II, 911, 969, 970; *NH*, p. 166.

15. Sir Kenelm Digby, *Private Memoirs of Sir Kenelm Digby*, ed. H. N. Nicholas (London, 1827), p. xxvi; see also *Biographia Britannica*, "Sir Kenelm Digby." Notice still another interesting parallel between these two men: Having just cited Digby, Hawthorne goes on to say that a rumor gained ground among the people about Chillingworth's sudden appearance—"that Heaven had wrought an absolute miracle, by transporting an eminent Doctor of Physic, from a German university, bodily through the air, and setting him down at the door of Mr. Dimmesdale's study!" (Pp. 148-149.) John Aubrey—*"Brief Lives and Other Selected Writings*, ed. Anthony Powell (New York, 1925), p. 44—makes a similar remark about Digby: "He was such a goodly handsome person . . . that had he been drop't out of the clowdes in any part of the world, he would have made himselfe respected."

16. There seems to be no record that Hawthorne knew this work, but he did like to read autobiographies. He once wrote to Fields: "Of all things I delight in autobiographies" (*Works*, XII, 531).

17. Digby, pp. 119-146.

18. Digby, p. 146.

19. Digby, pp. 137-138, 149-150.

20. *State Trials*, III, 576, 585.

21. *HM*, IV, 232-233.

22. Oldmixon, pp. 119, 128-129.

23. Preface to 1730 edition, *State Trials*, I, xxxvi.

24. *HM*, IV, 230.

25. "An Old Wife's Tale," "Old Esther Dudley," "Ethan Brand."

26. *State Trials*, II, 91; *HM*, VI, 66.

27. *State Trials*, II, 33; *NH*, p. 70.

28. Codrington, "The Life and Death of . . . Essex," *HM*, VI, 9; Amos, p. 52.

29. *NH*, "Epistle to Reader." See also Birch, *Court and Times*, I, 377; II, 143, 200; Violet A. Wilson, *Society Women in Shakespeare's Time* (New York, 1925), p. 205. On this whole subject of the feminist controversy, see

Wilson, pp. 205-212; Louis B. Wright, *Middle-Class Culture in Elizabethan England* (Chapel Hill, 1935), pp. 493, 499; and Chilton Latham Powell, *English Domestic Relations, 1487-1653* (New York, 1917), p. 162.

30. John Aubrey, *"Brief Lives" and Other Selected Writings*, ed. Anthony Powell (New York, 1949), p. 304. According to S. R. Gardiner in *DNB*, William Chillingworth (*q.v.*), like Roger Chillingworth, was also on speaking terms with Sir Kenelm Digby (*Works*, V, 148).

31. Edward Hyde, Earl of Clarendon, *The History of the Rebellion and Civil Wars in England,* A New Edition (Oxford, 1840), II, 510, 511.

32. William Chillingworth, *The Religion of Protestants a Safe Way to Salvation,* 2nd ed. (London, 1638), "Dedication" and p. 73.

33. Chillingworth, pp. 55-67.

34. Stewart, p. 100.

35. Kempe, p. 409.

36. Kempe, p. 411.

37. Kempe, p. 384.

38. *State Trials*, XIII, 1216, 1244.

39. *Gentleman's Magazine*, XXXIX, 54.

40. *Ibid.*, LXIII, 1055.

CHAPTER 11

1. Contrast Hawthorne's account of his failure to bring to light a literary treasure while living in the Old Manse (*Works*, II, 26, 29, 45). The situations described are very much alike: a rainy day, a remote upper-room, a search among old and faded documents of his predecessors. But in "The Old Manse" he reports that he could find no literary treasure, while in "The Custom House" his search is rewarded.

2. Joseph Barlow Felt in *The Annals of Salem* (Salem, 1827), p. 455, records the death of Jonathan Pue in the year 1760, but there is no mention that he was an antiquarian nor that he left any private papers on New England history.

3. Two other documents in *The Narrative History*, however, are not related to the Overbury case. One is "An Abstract or Brief Declaration of the Present State of His Majesties Revenew, with the Assignations and Defalcations upon the Same" (London, 1651). The other is "A True Relation of the Commissions and Warrants for the Condemnation and Burning of Bartholomew Legatt and Thomas Withman" (London, 1651). These tracts are parts III and IV of the *History*.

4. *NH*, "Epistle to Reader."

5. *HM*, V, 391.

6. *NH*, pp. 68-69.

7. See *Works*, I, 154, 164, 210, 218.

8. *NH*, p. 13.

9. *NH*, p. 51.

10. *NH*, p. 57.

11. *NH*, p. 65.

12. *NH*, p. 73.

13. *Works*, II, 27.

14. Hawthorne described in his journal in December, 1848, a nocturnal setting in his study into which ghosts might glide quietly (Stewart, p. 124). He appears to have recast these ideas in "The Custom House" (pp. 54-56). Niccols' description of midnight, the ghost-walking hour—the whole passage is not included here—could have recalled Hawthorne's own observations of a year earlier.

15. *HM*, III, 346.

16. *HM*, III, 351-352.

17. There is an analogy between this structure of a series of self-characterizations and what critics have called the tableau-like structure of the novel. Malcolm Cowley—*The Portable Hawthorne* (New York, 1948), pp. 18-19—characterizes the narrative movement as a series of balanced tableaus. Mark Van Doren — *Nathaniel Hawthorne*

(New York, 1949), p. 164—states that these tableaus are strikingly visualized and appear for the moment to bring everything to a standstill. The speech of each ghost in the poem creates, in effect, a little static picture as he rehearses his life and transgressions. These tableaus are tied together with brief narrative links. Though the levels of art are quite different, the structural rhythms are very much alike.

18. *HM*, III, 368.

19. Hawthorne had written in this style before the novel. "The Gray Champion" (1835) and "The Ambitious Guest" (1835) seem to employ the style without making the most of it. "The Minister's Black Veil" (1836) and "Lady Eleanor's Mantle" (1838) clearly anticipate the realization of the possibilities of this point of view. Prior to the novel, however, Hawthorne does not seem to have used the word *vulgar* in describing the people.

20. *NH*, p. 31.
21. *NH*, p. 31.
22. *NH*, p. 33.
23. *NH*, p. 61.
24. *NH*, p. 60.
25. *NH*, p. 69.
26. F. O. Matthiessen, *American Renaissance* (New York, 1941), pp. 276-277.
27. The device of multiple-choice explanations seems to appear first in Hawthorne's stylistic development in "The Gray Champion," *Works*, I, 30. Thereafter it is not uncommon to find it in several of his better tales: "The Minister's Black Veil," *Works*, I, 56; "The Prophetic Pictures," *Works*, I, 195; "Edward Randolph's Portrait," *Works*, I, 295-296.
28. *NH*, p. 25.
29. *NH*, pp. 31-32.
30. *NH*, p. 36.
31. *NH*, p. 50.
32. *NH*, pp. 53-54.

Chapter 12

1. Stewart, pp. lxvi-lxvii, lxxxix.
2. *Works*, II, 106-107.
3. *Works*, III, 447, 454-455.
4. Fields, pp. 49-51.
5. Bridge, pp. 110-112.
6. I am indebted to Lowes, *The Road to Xanadu*, especially pp. 430-431, for this interpretation of the creative operation.
7. Matthew 13:45-46.
8. "Preface" to *The Snow-Image and Other Twice-Told Tales* in *Works*, III, 386.
9. Fields, p. 52.

BIBLIOGRAPHY

I. MAJOR SOURCES OF *The Scarlet Letter*

The Harleian Miscellany; or, a Collection of Scarce, Curious, and Entertaining Pamphlets and Tracts, as well in Manuscript as in Print, Found in the Late Earl of Oxford's Library, Interspersed with Historical, Political, and Critical Notes (London, 1808-1811), III, 316-322; III, 344-368; V, 349-403.

Thomas Bayly Howell, ed., *A Complete Collection of State Trials and Proceedings for High Treason and Other Crimes and Misdemeanors from the Earliest Period to the Year 1783* (London, 1816), II, 786-862, 911-1022.

Alfred John Kempe, *The Loseley Manuscripts: Manuscripts, and Other Rare Documents, Illustrative of Some of the More Minute Particulars of English History, Biography, and Manners, from the Reign of Henry VIII to that of James I* (London, 1836), pp. 379-417.

[Michael Sparke, ed.], *The Narrative History of King James, for the First Fourteen Years* (London, 1651).

II. MINOR SOURCES OF *The Scarlet Letter*

Andrew Amos, *The Great Oyer of Poisoning: The Trial of the Earl of Somerset for the Poisoning of Sir Thomas Overbury, in the Tower of London* (London, 1846).

Biographia Britannica; or, the Lives of the Most Eminent Persons Who Have Flourished in Great Britain and Ireland, from the Earliest Ages down to the Present Times (London, 1746-1766), "Devereux," "Howard," "Overbury," "Russell."*

Thomas Birch, *The Court and Times of James the First; Containing a Series of Historical and Confidential Letters, in which Will Be Found a Detail of the Public Transactions and Events in Great Britain during That Period,* 2 vols. (London, 1849).

The Harleian Miscellany (London, 1808-1811), VI, 5-9.

John Oldmixon, *The History of England, during the Reigns of the Royal House of Stuart* (London, 1730).

Sir Anthony Weldon, *The Court and Character of King James* (London, 1651).

III. WORKS CONSULTED ON THE OVERBURY AFFAIR

The Dictionary of National Biography, ed. Sir Leslie Stephen and Sir Sidney Lee (London, 1937-1939), "Sir Thomas Overbury," "Robert Carr," "Sir Gervase Helwys."

Samuel R. Gardiner, *The History of England, 1603-1642,* (Boston, 1883), II, 166-187, 331-363.

Great Britain, Public Record Office, *Calendar of State Papers, Domestic Series, of the Reign of James I. 1611-1618,* ed. Mary Anne Everett Green (London, 1858).

* Various other encyclopedias, biographical and historical dictionaries, and sketches of English peers that were current in Hawthorne's day might well be added to this list in the future, but they were not available for this study.

Bibliography

Richard Niccols, *Sir Thomas Overbury's Vision* (Hunterian Club, No. XVII), ed. James Maidment (Glasgow, 1873).

Sir Thomas Overbury, *The Miscellaneous Works . . . of Sir Thomas Overbury,* ed. Edward F. Rimbault (London, 1856).

Edward Abbot Parry, *The Overbury Mystery: A Chronicle of Fact and Drama of the Law* (London, 1925).

Charles Whibley, *Essays in Biography* (London, 1913).

IV. WORKS CONSULTED ON SEVENTEENTH-CENTURY HISTORY

John Aubrey, *"Brief Lives" and Other Selected Writings,* ed. Anthony Powell (New York, 1949).

William Chillingworth, *The Religion of Protestants a Safe Way to Salvation,* 2nd ed. (London, 1638).

Edward Hyde, Earl of Clarendon, *The History of the Rebellion and Civil War in England,* A New Edition, 2 vols. (Oxford, 1840).

Sir Kenelm Digby, *Private Memoirs of Sir Kenelm Digby,* ed. H. N. Nicholas (London, 1827).

Joseph Barlow Felt, *The Annals of Salem, from its First Settlement* (Salem, 1827).

Thomas Frankland, *Annals of King James I and King Charles I* (London, 1681).

The Harleian Miscellany (London, 1808-1811), IV, 220-238.

Cotton Mather, *The Wonders of the Invisible World,* ed. John Offer (London, 1862).

Chilton Latham Powell, *English Domestic Relations, 1487-1653* (New York, 1917).

Violet A. Wilson, *Society Women in Shakespeare's Time* (New York, 1925).

John Winthrop, *Winthrop's Journal "History of New England," 1630-1649* (Original Narratives of Early American History), ed. James Kendall Hosmer, 2 vols. (New York, 1908).

Louis B. Wright, *Middle-Class Culture in Elizabethan England* (Chapel Hill, 1935).

V. WRITINGS BY AND ABOUT NATHANIEL HAWTHORNE

Horatio Bridge, *Personal Recollections of Nathaniel Hawthorne* (New York, 1893).

Malcolm Cowley, *The Portable Hawthorne* (New York, 1948).

James T. Fields, *Yesterdays with Authors* (Boston, 1900).

Nathaniel Hawthorne, *The Complete Works of Nathaniel Hawthorne,* ed. George Parsons Lathrop (Riverside Edition), 12 vols. (Boston, 1890).

Marion L. Kesselring, *Hawthorne's Reading, 1828-1850: A Transcription and Identification of Titles Recorded in the Charge-Books of the Salem Athenaeum* (New York, 1949).

F. O. Matthiessen, *American Renaissance: Art and Expression in the Age of Emerson and Whitman* (New York, 1941).

Frank Preston Stearns, *The Life and Genius of Nathaniel Hawthorne* (Boston, 1906).

Randall Stewart, *The American Notebooks by Nathaniel Hawthorne* (New Haven, 1933).

——————, *Nathaniel Hawthorne: A Biography* (New Haven, 1948).

——————, "Recollections of Hawthorne by His Sister Elizabeth," *American Literature,* XVI (January, 1945), pp. 316-331.

Mark Van Doren, *Nathaniel Hawthorne* (New York, 1949).

INDEX

147

Index

vorce from Essex, 2-3, 13, 54, 76; marriage to Carr, 3; birth of girl in prison, 3, 14-15, 48; baby taken from her, 15, 24-25; trial for murder, 15-16, 18, 19; prison confinement of, 19-20; vow of revenge on Overbury, 20-21; isolation of, 22-24; long hair of at wedding, 38-39; loathsome death of, 44-45; witchcraft of, 51-52, 53; ruse of virginity of, 54; and Anne Turner, 2-3, 5, 13, 17, 48, 52, 53, 56, 74, 78. *See also* Hester Prynne

ILLNESS, LANGUISHING, 4, 29-30, 39
Irving, Washington, 102

JAMES I, KING: suspected in murder of Overbury, 3; licentiousness of reign, 4; and Carr, 5; death of, 4; role of in Lady Frances' divorce proceedings, 76-77; mentioned, 1, 93, 97, 108

KNOLLYS, LADY CATHERINE (sister of Lady Frances), 24

LATHROP, GEORGE P., 9
Laud, Archbishop William, 96
Loseley Hall: and Bellingham's hall, 83-84, 87
Loseley Manuscripts, The, 7-8, 102, 112
Lowes, John Livingston, 10

MANWARING, ARTHUR, 13, 93
Marriage, unhappy: of Hester and Lady Frances, 53-54
Massachusetts, 10
Mather, Cotton, 75
Medical studies: of Chillingworth and Franklin, 66-68
Milton, John, 132

NAMES, SYMBOLISM OF, 96-100, 126-130
Narrative History, The, 5-6, 102-103, 111, 112, 133
Needlework: of Hester and Anne Turner, 48, 49
Niccols, Richard, 4, 5-6; and Pue, 106-108, 133

Northampton, Henry Howard, Earl of, 13, 19
Noye, William, 8, 92

OATH OF SECRECY, 20-22, 36-38, 122
Overbury, Sir Thomas: murder of, 1; cited in *The Scarlet Letter*, 1, 31, 46, 112; protests marriage of Carr, 2; imprisoned, 2; friend and counselor to Carr, 26-27; poisoning of, 33; reputation of, 57-58; bodily marks of, 59-62; poem of, "The Wife," 97. *See also* Dimmesdale

PEARL: birth of in prison, 14-15; on scaffold, 15; retained by Hester, 24; heiress of Chillingworth, 43-44; noble marriage of, 44; and Una Hawthorne, 70-71; symbolism of name, 99, 127-128; formation of, 123
Point of view, popular, 108-111
Prison, Boston: and Tower of London, 81-82
Private Memoirs of Sir Kenelm Digby, 94-96
Prynne, Hester. *See* Hester Prynne
Prynne, William, 96-97, 126-127
Pue, Jonathan, 1, 101, 103, 105-106, 108, 134

RALEIGH, SIR WALTER, 5, 97
Reprobation: of Chillingworth and Franklin, 68-69, 125, 126
Royal Society of London, 93

SALEM ATHENAEUM, 7, 8
Salvation: of Dimmesdale and Helwyse, 42-43, 62-64; of Hester and Anne Turner, 54-56, 125; of Overbury, 63-64
Savage, Richard, 9
Scaffold: Hester on, 13-19; night scene on, 35-36; confessions on, of Dimmesdale and Helwyse, 40-41
Scarlet letter, 9-10, 12, 18, 48-50, 56, 118-119
Scarlet Letter, The: source ascribed to Pue, 1; allusions to Overbury in, 1, 31; idea for, 10; completion of, 8, 118; genesis and evolution of, 118-123

149

Index

Scott, Sir Walter, 8, 102

Shakespeare, William, 132

"Sir Thomas Overbury's Vision," 5-6, 105-108, 133

Somerset, Robert Carr, Earl of. *See* Carr, Robert

Sparke, Michael, 7, 96, 102, 104-105

Spenser, Edmund, 127

Spiritualization of sources, 116-117, 123-124

State Trials, 4, 6-7, 102

Stewart, Randall, 114

Suffolk, Thomas Howard, Earl of, 19

Supernatural, 84-86, 94-95

Symbolism: of long hair, 38-39; of scarlet letter, 51, 59; of bodily marks, 59-60; of crooked shoulder, 65; of ruff, 103; of setting, 130; of names, 96-100, 126-130

THEMES, 124-126

Tower of London, 1, 3, 81-82

Turner, Anne: cited in *The Scarlet Letter*, 1, 4, 74; inventor of yellow ruff, 1-2, 49-50, 103; friend of Lady Frances, 3, 13, 74 (*See also* Howard, Frances); adultery of, 13; complicity of in Overbury murder, 21-22; repentance of, 37, 55-56; needlework skill of, 49; pride and vanity of, 51; witchcraft of, 52; married to physician, 52-53; and Mistress Hibbins, 72-74

WESTON, RICHARD, 3, 66, 73, 82

Whiting, Mr., 18

Wilson, John, 17, 99, 126, 127

Winthrop, Governor John, 80, 126

Winwood, Sir Ralph, 3

Witchcraft, 5, 13, 32, 33, 51, 52, 53, 72-73, 74, 75-77

Wonders of the Invisible World, The, 75-76

Woodfall, William, 9

YELLOW RUFF, 1-2, 49-50, 74, 97, 103, 118-119

150

DATE DUE

JAN 3 1967	OCT 2 9 1984		
JAN 18 1967	MAY 2 1985		
APR 24 1967	JUN 3 1986		
JAN 19 1968	FEB 2 1987		
JUL 9 '68	2-10-87		
AUG 1 1969	NOV 25 1991		
OCT 5 1970	FEB 10 1992		
OCT 11 1972			
OCT 27 1972	FEB 2 3 1994		
NOV 14 '72	3-11-94-R		
APR 30 '73	MAY 12 1995		
MAR 24 '75	JUN 1 2001		
DEC 14 '75	FEB 01 2001		
MAR '76			
NOV 21 '77			
JUN 25 1984			
GAYLORD			PRINTED IN U.S.A.